VISUAL AND MULTIMODAL URBAN SOCIOLOGY, PART B

RESEARCH IN URBAN SOCIOLOGY

Series Editor: Ray Hutchison

Volumes:

RESEARCH IN URBAN SOCIOLOGY   VOLUME 18B

VISUAL AND MULTIMODAL URBAN SOCIOLOGY, PART B: EXPLORING THE URBAN EVERYDAY

EDITED BY

LUC PAUWELS
University of Antwerp, Belgium

United Kingdom – North America – Japan
India – Malaysia – China

Emerald Publishing Limited
Howard House, Wagon Lane, Bingley BD16 1WA, UK

First edition 2023

Reprints and permissions service
Contact: permissions@emeraldinsight.com

British Library Cataloguing in Publication Data
A catalogue record for this book is available from the British Library

ISBN: 978-1-80455-633-7 (Print)
ISBN: 978-1-80455-632-0 (Online)
ISBN: 978-1-80455-634-4 (Epub)

ISSN: 1047-0042 (Series)

Printed and bound by CPI Group (UK) Ltd, Croydon, CR0 4YY

INVESTOR IN PEOPLE

CONTENTS

LIST OF FIGURES

ABOUT THE CONTRIBUTORS

Jim Brogden is the Director of Practice Research in the School of Media and Communication at the University of Leeds. He is the author of *Photography and the Non-Place: The Cultural Erasure of the City* (Palgrave, 2019), and co-author with Stephen Coleman of *Capturing the Mood of Democracy: The British General Election 2019* (Palgrave, 2020). He is a member of the International Visual Sociology Association, a Fellow of the Royal Society of Arts, United Kingdom, and visiting professor at the American Academy of Art College, Chicago. Contact: School of Media and Communication, University of Leeds, Woodhouse Lane, Leeds LS2 9JT, UK.

Stephen Coleman is Professor of Political Communication in the School of Media and Communication at the University of Leeds. He has written several books, including *How Voters Feel* (2013) and *How People Talk About Politics* (2020). He is interested in exploring the concept of socio-political mood.

Saskia I. de Wit is Assistant Professor at the Section of Landscape Architecture, Delft University of Technology, the Netherlands. She combines teaching and research with practice at her own firm *Saskia de Wit tuin en landschap*. Her research focuses on the garden as a core concept of the field of landscape architecture, as expressed in her publication *Hidden Landscapes. The Metropolitan Garden as a Multisensory Expression of Place* (2018) which ties the concept of the enclosed garden as an articulation of landscape to contemporary metropolitan developments. The concept of the garden is used as a lens for further research into the urban landscape, leftover spaces and the (multi-sensory) perception of place. Currently she is involved in researching urban forestry from the spatial-experiential perspective.

Paolo Silvio Harald Favero is an anthropologist and artist with an interest for the meaning of images in human life. He works across visual and digital cultures, anthropology and art. His most recent project focusses on dying, living and loving in New Delhi. Paolo is also specialised in emerging technologies, visual and sensory ethnography, arts-based methods and existential anthropology. He is the author of four single-authored books: *Image-Making-India: Visual Culture, Technology, Politics* (Routledge, 2020), *The Present Image: Visible Stories in a Digital Habitat* (Palgrave Macmillan, 2018), *Dentro e Oltre l'Immagine: saggi sulla cultura visiva e politica nell'Italia contemporanea* (Meltemi 2017), and *India Dreams: Cultural Identity Among Young Middle Class Men in New Delhi* (Stockholm University Press 2005). He is Professor of Visual and Digital Culture at the University of Antwerp where he is a member of the Visual and Digital Cultures Research Center (ViDi).

Annalisa Frisina is Associate Professor of Sociology at the Department FISPPA (Philosophy, Sociology, Education and Applied Psychology) of the University of Padova, where she teaches qualitative and visual methods for undergraduate, graduate and doctoral students. Her main research interests are in sociology of racism and migrations, from a post and decolonial perspective. Her participatory video "Decolonising the City. Visual Dialogues in Padova" received two Visual Research Awards in 2021, by the International Visual Sociology Association (AntiColonial and AntiRacist Award for Visual Activism) and by the Festival DocuCity/MetiCittà, University of Milan, in cooperation with the Museum of Cultures. Among her publications are a book on *Visual Research and Socio-cultural Transformations* (UTET 2013), an edited book on *Visual Methods* (Il Mulino 2016) and her latest book on *Contemporary Racisms. Sociological Perspectives* (Carocci 2020). Among her recent research essays (with S. A. Kyeremeh) are *Music and Words Against Racism. A Qualitative Study With Racialized Artists in Italy*, in Ethnic and Racial Studies (2022) and *Art and Counter-Racialization Processes. A Qualitative Research Journey With Italy's Illegitimate Children*, in Studi Culturali (2021).

Luc Pauwels is Professor Emeritus of Visual Sociology and Anthropology at the University of Antwerp (Faculty of Social Sciences), Founding and former Director of the Visual and Digital Cultures Research Center (ViDi) and currently President of the 'Visual Sociology' Research Committee of the International Sociological Association (ISA). He is also a former Vice-President of the International Visual Sociology Association (IVSA), of the International Visual Literacy Association (IVLA) as well as a Past Chair of the Visual Communication Studies Division of the International Communication Association (ICA). Books include: *Visual Cultures of Science: Rethinking Representational Practices in Knowledge Building and Science Communication* (2006, Dartmouth College Press, UPNE), *Reframing Visual Social Science. Towards a More Visual Sociology and Anthropology* (2015, Cambridge University Press) and *The SAGE Handbook of Visual Research Methods* (2011, 1st ed. with E. Margolis; 2020, 2nd ed. with D. Mannay).

David Schalliol is an Associate Professor of Sociology at St. Olaf College who is interested in the relationship between community, social structure, and place. He exhibits widely, including in the Chicago Architecture Biennial, the Centre Régional de la Photographie Hauts-de-France, and the Museum of Contemporary Photography. His work has been supported by institutions including the Graham Foundation and the European Union and featured in publications including *MAS Context, The New York Times*, and *Social Science Research*. David is the author of *Isolated Building Studies* (UTAKATADO) and co-author, with Michael Carriere, of *The City Creative: The Rise of Urban Placemaking in Contemporary America* (The University of Chicago Press). He additionally contributes to such films as *Almost There* (Kartemquin Films) and *Highrise: Out*

My Window (National Film Board of Canada), which won an International Digital Emmy for Non-Fiction. His directorial debut, *The Area,* premiered at the Full Frame Documentary Film Festival and has aired on *America Reframed* and PBS.org. David earned his BA from Kenyon College and his MA and PhD from The University of Chicago.

Giovanni Semi is Associate Professor of Sociology at the Interuniversity Department of Regional and Urban Studies and Planning of the University of Turin where he coordinates the PhD program in Sociology and Methodology of Social Research at the universities of Milan and Turin. He splits his research interests in two main but interrelated domains: urban studies and multicultural analysis. He has extensively worked on gentrification dynamics, housing studies and urban marketplaces, with a special interest in the qualitative analysis of class and racial segregations. Semi has extensively published in journals such as *Identities, Environment and Planning A, Ethnologie Française*, and in collective works in English, French and Italian. He has a kid and a dog and holds a double PhD from EHESS-Paris and Università di Torino.

Jon Wagner is Professor Emeritus in the School of Education at the University of California, Davis. His current interests include visual communication (from illuminated manuscripts to YouTube videos), the phenomenology of Alzheimer's care, the 'visual commons' and community narratives. His previous work focused on children's material culture, qualitative and visual research methods, school change and the social and philosophical foundations of education. He authored *Misfits and Missionaries: A School for Black Dropouts* (1977) and edited *Images of Information: Still Photography in the Social Sciences* (1979) and 'Seeing Kids' Worlds' an issue of *Visual Sociology* (1999). He is a past president of the International Visual Sociology Association and was founding image editor of the journal *Contexts* (2001–2004).

INTRODUCTION TO "VISUAL AND MULTIMODAL URBAN SOCIOLOGY, PART B: EXPLORING THE URBAN EVERYDAY"

Luc Pauwels

Volume 18B in the *Research in Urban Sociology* series is the second part of a cross-disciplinary exploration of a more visual and multimodal urban sociology. The double volume 18A and 18B explores cross-disciplinary ways in which the city and city life may be approached, studied, and expressed through visual and multimodal means and methods, thereby as much as possible including sensory experiences other than those related to seeing and hearing.

1. LOOKING BACK AT PART A: IMAGINING THE SENSORY CITY

The first part of *Visual and Multimodal Urban Sociology* (Volume 18A of the *Research in Urban Sociology* series) sets the scene for both volumes and focuses on ways and technologies to interrogate and relive the urban past as well as to navigate the present. A brief synopsis of these preceding chapters may offer the reader of this second volume an idea of what is covered in the first part of this double volume.

The first chapter of Volume 18A titled "Viewing and Sensing the City: Cross-Disciplinary Perspectives, Methods, and Technologies" by Luc Pauwels discusses the thematic focus of the two new volumes as well as their grounding in different established and emerging disciplines and traditions. It does so by elaborating on the differences and interconnections of visual sociology and urban sociology in their quest to understand human settlements, and it argues for expanding the focus to other disciplines that are equally geared toward

Visual and Multimodal Urban Sociology, Part B
Research in Urban Sociology, Volume 18B, 1–6
Copyright © 2023 by Emerald Publishing Limited
All rights of reproduction in any form reserved
ISSN: 1047-0042/doi:10.1108/S1047-00422023000018B010

researching aspects of the city in visual and multimodal ways. The second chapter, "Imagining the City as Home: Functional prerequisites and moral challenges" by John Grady, then presents a substantial treatise about what defines a city and how to approach this visually. It provides a comprehensive framework for looking at various aspects and prerequisites of cities as core human settlements. The third chapter "Unpacking Urban Life in the Past. 'Time Machine' as a Data Visualization and Analysis Tool," by Danielle van den Heuvel and Julia Noordegraaf, presents the "Time Machine," an unmatched repository of information and a remarkably advanced visualization tool to investigate different interconnected aspects of urban life in their visual and spatial context. The fourth chapter, "Georeferencing Early Photographic Studios and Using Historic Photographs to Study Urban Processes and Environments," by Jeremy Rowe, provides important new insight into New York–based photography businesses in the mid-nineteenth century and contemplates the potential and hazards of using "found images" to study the urban context. The fifth chapter, "Playing the Early Renaissance City," by Ray Hutchison, investigates to what extent games can impart knowledge about a city's culture and how to navigate it, through analyzing the popular *Assassin's Creed* series set in early Renaissance Florence. The sixth and final chapter of Volume 18A, "Learning from Street View: Lessons in Urban Visuality," by Scott McQuire, offers a critical but balanced evaluation of Google Street View and Google Maps as key digital infrastructures in today's knowledge production of the urban context.

2. AN OVERVIEW OF PART B: EXPLORING THE URBAN EVERYDAY

The present, second, part devoted to *Visual and Multimodal Urban Sociology* hosts a further seven chapters, this time with an emphasis on methods and concrete applications of these methods in the form of rich visual and multimodal ethnographies on different aspects of everyday life in cities. Obviously, there are many intersections between chapters from both volumes, as most chapters combine a discussion and application of methods, disciplinary foci and technologies with a certain thematic interest.

Chapter 1, "Visually Exploring the Globalizing City: From Data Visualizations to 'In Situ' Approaches," discusses different options for researching globalization and cultural change in cities. It starts by examining key debates on globalization as a multifaceted and contested phenomenon and interrogating the predominantly quantitative approaches and visualizations of this phenomenon. Acting upon the limitations of these high-level and generic operationalizations and representations of globalization, I provide in this chapter a systematic overview of visual methods to interrogate the visual dimensions of globalization processes as expressed in material culture elements of a varied nature, as well as through visible and recordable aspects of human behavior in urban public spaces. This varied array of methods ranges from collecting and analyzing existing or "found" visual data from a variety of sources, to the purposeful production of visual materials by the researcher in an exploratory, random, or systematic fashion, to using visual materials to elicit responses from respondents or to asking respondents to produce visual materials in response to a research assignment. Finally, researchers may choose to use their visual materials and skills to share their findings and insights in novel, more experimental, and experiential formats. Visual approaches to globalization and cultural exchanges – in particular those based on "in situ" observations and experiences – may help to enrich and complement the more abstract discourse of globalization and transnationalism with empirically grounded and localized insights regarding concrete expressions and enactments of cultural encounters in urban settings. Obviously these methods can be used for researching most other aspects of urban life, as exemplified by several chapters in this volume.

Chapter 2, "Perception in Motion: Alternative Research Techniques for Exploring the Urban Landscape," by Saskia I. de Wit, adds very important dimensions and insights to the study of the built environment as a site of analysis, capable of not just triggering visual but also a host of other sensory sensations. The author proposes several notation or scoring techniques to represent both the visual and the nonvisual qualities of moving through the many ephemeral aspects of the urban environment, thus providing the means to communicate the complex experiential potential of a constructed environment. To generate these scores, human subjects need to walk through designated urban spaces and record their multisensory dynamic impressions: what they see, hear, smell, and feel as they move along. Walking indeed constitutes a central way of experiencing a city and, as such, an embodied way of knowing. However, human subjects moving through space is for de Wit, in fact, just a device to "score" the field and to construct a more or less objective map of what the "place holds" in terms of sensory cues. Whereas many scholars will concentrate on how the environment is "processed" by individuals, this landscape architect chooses to concentrate on "unearthing" the formal traits of the perceived urban landscape and how these elements can be shaped to trigger certain actions and perceptions. De Wit also reminds us of the care needed when producing (visual) representations, as to an important extent they will determine the validity of the ensuing analysis.

In Chapter 3, "The Visual Commons: Where Residents Become Neighbors," Jon Wagner introduces the concept of a "visual commons," which emerged from his earlier involvement with community studies and theories, as well as from his visual ethnography spanning more than four decades of his neighborhood, "Thousand Oaks" in Berkeley, California. For over 45 years, Wagner photographed, as a participant-observer, numerous aspects of his changing neighborhood including streets and sidewalks, spaces in between, garbage bins, automobiles, houses, and vegetation, as well as resident wildlife – in short, anything that might help him understand "how people see where they live." He describes in great detail his encounter with the changing neighborhood as well as his intellectual journey toward conceptualizing this new idea. Wagner's concept of the "visual commons" seeks to confront existing visible features of a neighborhood with what residents make of it and care about. This could not be accomplished by just looking at the researcher-produced images but also involved talking with the residents to bring about their imaginaries of the neighborhood and the issues that bring them together or set them apart. Through combining etic and emic approaches, Wagner was able to conceptualize the visual commons as a "workspace" that exists "in both resident imaginations and social interaction." This image-rich chapter offers a detailed longitudinal study of a particular neighborhood, while at the same time developing and applying an important new concept for community studies and urban sociology.

Chapter 4, "Burned out: A Visual and Lyrical Sociology of Smoking in the City," by Stephen Coleman and Jim Brogden, presents a microbehavioral ethnographic study of a noteworthy but largely taken-for-granted practice and social phenomenon, using two complementary methods: in-depth interviewing and researcher-produced photographs. The researchers embarked on this study by walking in the city center of Leeds to investigate the social practice of taking a break to smoke. They started conversations with smokers and vapers outside of corporate buildings and these interviews quickly moved beyond talking about the physical need for nicotine. More than the very act of smoking, these moments of going outside meant a needed break from the hectic rhythm of work life. During the many excursions in the city, photographs were made which provided evidence of individual smokers as "unique urban protagonists" and they also documented the place where these individuals chose to position themselves, possibly offering indications as to 'why', for example to seek a safe secluded spot, or a vantage point from which to observe, or to make contact with others. Coleman and Brogden discovered that besides the obvious act of smoking, these breaks were ascribed by the workers as moments for reflection, meditation, and for reconnecting to the city and the world. The main rationale of this "street-level" study was to explore: "how one such seemingly empty act of passing time reflects urban aspirations that are broader and deeper than are visible at first sight," but then also to raise "questions about how else urban cultures could make room for these vital human activities." This team of scholars, one a political scientist and the other a photography scholar, produced with this chapter another stellar example of a lyrical multimodal ethnography, integrating brilliantly phrased observations and reflections with equally important expressive photography.

In Chapter 5, "What We See, and What We Do Not: Resignifying Urban Traces of Colonialism," Giovanni Semi and Annalisa Frisina joined forces to address the crucial issue of visibility versus invisibility, or the presence and effects of "visibility regimes." Visibility regimes refer to the power held by dominant groups about what can be seen and how it should be seen, and as a corollary, what is purposefully left out of view, hidden, or aestheticized. Emancipatory actions therefore involve to an important extent a struggle for "visibility" and a breaking of silence, a legitimate striving to leave a state of invisibility or of being muted, to finally become seen and heard. The first part of the chapter discusses consecutive forms of urbanism, each characterized by a distinct visibility regime: the Fordist era with an emphasis on industrial manufacturing, the post-Fordist period with an emphasis on creating "cosmopolitan and sanitized public spaces, safe and purified from any form of conflict," and the emerging "platform urbanism" through to the accelerated process of mediated experiences and networks, which create other forms of inequality and (in)visibility. The second part then applies the theoretical framing of the urban context as a site where visibility and invisibility are enacted, to the issue of decolonization and racism as arguably one of its more apparent instantiations. It describes a research project that Frisina conducted with her students to bring forward the "counter memories" of six Italian Afro-descendants by asking them to share their stories and reactions to traces of colonialisms (monuments, streets, shop names, etc.) in the streets of Padua. The project involved the production of a participatory video (titled: "Decolonizing the city. Visual dialogues in Padova"), the production of "counter images" by the interlocutors for display in the city, and walking methods. This chapter reminds us that visual research also involves being attentive to what is missing in the visible world, through performing a form of "negative" or reversed analysis of what is not in plain sight and why.

Chapter 6, "For an 'Expanded' Visual/Sensory Ethnography: Co-Living With Death in New Delhi," by Paolo Silvio Harald Favero, is aside from an intimate ethnographic account of a city, a rich and multilayered reflection on visual and multimodal research, or the ways in which established and emerging technologies are redefining and expanding the act of being among people, developing rapport, and capturing and sharing their unique views on life. Focusing on death as an intricate part of life in New Delhi, and in particular in connection with its unmatched degree of air pollution, the author vividly describes his encounters with fascinating people who are at the brink of death or at least preparing themselves for it. Balancing between ethnography and autoethnography, Paolo Favero shares his personal experiences with death and grieving as a way to connect with the research participants and prefers to see his interlocutors as "guides" in his quest for understanding important aspects of life and death. Exploring the agency of emerging visual and multisensory technologies and their largely unchartered research potential, Favero clearly emphasizes the need to abandon the too easily made distinctions between mediated and nonmediated events or online and offline presences, and instead to put more effort into qualifying the nature and intersections of different forms of mediation and how they amalgamate within a continuous space of living. In his diverse attempts to connect with aspects of death and grieving, he uses a combination of technologies to explore different sensory experiences, which he presents as a form of "expanded" ethnography. He uses a variety of filming techniques, allowing for serendipity rather than preplanned scenarios. But he also makes ample use of photography – and in particular portrait photography – as a participatory process to intimately connect with his interlocutors.

Chapter 7 concludes this second volume of *Visual and Multimodal Urban Sociology* in a very visual manner with an approach or format that has been discussed in Chapter 1 as the "visual essay." David Schalliol's contribution "Isolated Buildings as Indicators of Social Change: A Visual Essay" indeed invites the reader, after being provided with some factual information on the depicted sites and their changes, to take an active stance and explore the many instances of solitary houses as markers of urban renewal or decay in Chicago's landscape of economic and racial segregation. The separate photographs may point to particular instances of neighborhood change and prompt the viewer to look for answers in the depicted environment about whether this is a first new building in a gentrifying neighborhood or the last stand in a decaying, divested environment. However, the full set of images (over 700 photographs which have been exhibited on various occasions) truly reveals the magnitude of this phenomenon. A series of separate depictions of isolated dwellings in deserted surroundings is followed by "thumbnail" panels or grid spreads, to entice readers to further explore the connections between these somewhat eerie remnants and the powers that shaped them. Both the informational and esthetic qualities of the photographs merit careful study and will prompt the viewer to ask questions, not only about individual cases, but through the accumulation of similar instances, about the more generic social, political, and economic mechanisms behind them. While visual scholars are not usually expected to be proficient in all aspects of the medium they are studying or employing, including the ability to produce images that excel in combining their mimetic and expressive potentials, this contribution exemplifies what may happen when a sociology professor proves to be in equal measure an accomplished photographer.

3. POSTSCRIPT

The contributions of both volumes of *Visual and Multimodal Urban Sociology*, varied and enlightening as they are in their own right, will gain more prominence by interconnecting to the overall quest of how to expand our knowledge of the urban through the use of multiple senses, established and emerging technologies, and ways to integrate the spatial and temporal dimension, and by grounding these efforts in solid – possibly hybrid and eclectic – theoretical frameworks and practicable methodologies. The contours and concrete realizations of "more visual, multimodal and cross-disciplinary" urban studies, as discussed here, are not presented as clearly delineated and comprehensive proposals but as indications of new frontiers to be explored.

Chapter 1

VISUALLY EXPLORING GLOBALIZING CITIES: FROM DATA VISUALIZATIONS TO 'IN SITU' APPROACHES

Luc Pauwels

ABSTRACT

Globalization, the ever-increasing worldwide flow of ideas, practices, and material objects resulting in increasing interdependency between people and nations across the globe, has numerous interrelated economic, political, cultural, ideological, environmental, and technological facets.

In an effort to make the elusive and multifaceted concept of globalization more tangible and measurable, different instruments have been developed, usually in the form of "indexes" based on quantitative data. These indexes mainly result in rankings of individual cities as well as whole countries with respect to their supposed level of globalization. Some items of the existing indexes to measure the level of globalization of nation states or cities refer to phenomena that are to some extent visually observable, but many aspects and manifestations of globalization escape these rather crude operationalizations.

Visual approaches to globalization help to enrich and complement the more abstract and mainly quantitatively supported discourses around this multifaceted phenomenon. They may provide valid and unobtrusive ways to assess and understand the impact of culture and cultural exchange in the daily lives of inhabitants of cities around the world and add a unique "localized," cross-cultural empirical perspective to the many divergent views and discussions about the presumed beneficial or detrimental nature of these processes. An 'in situ' visual approach to globalization may help to uncover the "real life" impact and the specific contexts of these processes at different locations. This

Visual and Multimodal Urban Sociology, Part B
Research in Urban Sociology, Volume 18B, 7–38
Copyright © 2023 by Emerald Publishing Limited
ISSN: 1047-0042/doi:10.1108/S1047-00422023000018B001

chapter discusses different options for researching globalization and cultural change in cities.

Keywords: Data visualization; globalization index; participatory visual methods; repeat photography; visual analysis; visual essay; visual methods

1. INTRODUCTION: A VISUAL APPROACH TO GLOBAL EVERYDAY LIFE

This chapter interrogates the visual dimensions of globalization processes as expressed in material culture elements of a varied nature, as well as through visible and recordable aspects of human behavior in urban public spaces. It seeks to enrich and complement the more abstract discourse of globalization and transnationalism with empirically grounded insights regarding concrete expressions and enactments of cultural encounters in urban contexts.

While communication scholars have taken an interest in the (visual) study of globalization processes, they have so far focused predominantly on mass-mediated expressions (films, advertisements, and TV programs) and more recently on social media and new media technologies (YouTube, Twitter, Flickr, Instagram, and Facebook). However, the actual sites where globalization takes place have received far less attention as concrete expressions of globalization. A study of globalization as experienced every day should definitely comprise aspects that are not premediated by mass media (behavior in public spaces and "grass-roots expressions" such as graffiti and other signs of resistance or appropriation). Such a view "on the ground and in the open" may finally complement the dominant narrower mass media–focused and quantitative discourses on globalization.

This chapter will therefore focus on how to research the visible expression of this meeting of values, norms, and expectations in the public realm of the rich "hubs of culture" that metropolitan areas typically are and thus try to fill a void in the study of globalization and cultural exchange as it is enacted and experienced every day.

As media scholar Aiello (2011) astutely notes: "the urban built environment is not only a central dimension of the mediatization and overall semioticization of everyday life, but also a form and force of mediation in its own right." It is no less than a "fundamental context for the negotiation of local and global(izing) identities" (Gendelman & Aiello, 2010).

Visual methods and techniques may take on a more central – though not exclusive – role in the effort to shed light on some unexplored and underexposed avenues of globalization and cultural exchange by focusing on the key roles played by city dwellers, urban planners, designers, advertisers, commercial forces, cultural institutions, local authorities, tourists, artists, protesters etc., as social agents in the (re)production of these cultural processes on a day-to-day basis. Visual methods, with their focus on observable and unspoken aspects of society, have the capacity to uncover immaterial traits of society (norms, values, and expectations) by looking carefully at material artifacts as cultural expressions and at visual practices and performances of people.

2. GLOBALIZATION AS A MULTIDIMENSIONAL PHENOMENON: ASPECTS AND CONTROVERSIES

Globalization, the ever-increasing worldwide flow of ideas, practices, and material objects boosted by organizations and transnational institutions and resulting in increasing interdependency between people and nations across the globe, is not a phenomenon that can simply be applauded or rejected. This transformation toward an intensified global interconnectivity has numerous interrelated economic, political, cultural, ideological, environmental, and technological facets (Lechner & Boli, 2005; Steger, 2014).

Though in many people's minds globalization is mainly a process of "Westernization" and more specifically "Americanization," this narrow view is no longer adequate. While brands such as Coca Cola, Starbucks, Google, and Amazon continue to figure as the most visible icons of globalization, many products, ideas, religions, and ways of life from other parts of the world are also spreading at a rapid pace. The current global market empire is clearly characterized by geopolitical multipolarity (McMichael, 2017). Today, globalization refers to the "myriad forms of connectivity and flows linking the local (and national) to the global – as well as the West to the East, and the North to the South" (Steger, 2014, p. 2).

Scholars, as well as political actors, activists, and the general public are rightfully divided and ambivalent as to the nature and impact of globalization and its effects on national and ethnic cultures and on humanity as a whole. Fierce debates reveal many divergent views with respect to its origins, scale, causation, effects, and outcomes.

Disputes on globalization tend to center around economic aspects, while the broader cultural dimensions of globalization processes receive less consideration.

More focused, localized, and diversified empirical research is needed to untangle and examine the multiple, unanticipated, and even seemingly contradictory effects of some processes of cultural exchange and their presumed hegemonic, homogenizing, or heterogenizing aspects.

While several aspects of globalization have consequences ranging from less desirable to devastating ones (enlargement of the poverty gap, cultural mainstreaming, unmitigated consumerism, ecological calamities), global problems (e.g., climate change, forced migration, economic crises, poverty, and armed conflicts) nevertheless need global solutions, implying transnational efforts and different forms of solidarity, and thus forms of interconnectivity.

Three paradigms or positions seem to dominate the discussion on globalization, each of which involve a different take on the phenomenon: *differentialism* – emphasizing barriers between cultures, which reject cultural flows to some degree, up to polarization and culture clashes; *hybridization* – emphasizing the integration of local and global flows (cf. the *glocalization* idea below); and *convergence* – emphasizing the growing similarities ("homogenization") between cultures as a result of exposure to the cultural flows (Nederveen Pieterse, 1996; Ritzer & Atalay, 2010).

Nederveen Pieterse (2015), for one, does not subscribe to the idea that we are currently experiencing a "clash of civilizations" (cf. Huntington, 1993) and he also challenges the view that globalization invariably leads to cultural homogenization. In contrast, he posits that we are witnessing the emergence of a "global mélange culture" as a result of varied processes of blending and hybridization. This assessment suggests a more positive outlook on the possible outcomes of globalization, one where identities are transformed but not eradicated and conflicts may still be contained.

A similar mildly positive view on the effects of globalization as a process of hybridization rather than homogenization is the concept of *glocalization* (Robertson, 1995), which refers to unique manifestations and blends of the global and the local in specific geographical areas. However, others have reacted to this rather optimistic view, which may indeed conceal the sometimes very invasive and imperialistic influence of powerful agents of globalization (nations, corporations, and lobbyists) on local cultures, as an instance of globalization for which Ritzer (2003) uses the term *grobalization*, which is further exemplified by his term "McDonaldization," (Ritzer, 2009). Thornton (2000) likewise opposes the seemingly unproblematic concept of *glocalization* as it "may too easily resolve the critical tension between global and local values" and thus legitimize the outcome while suppressing any opposition.

Different perspectives on (aspects of) globalization not only reveal widely divergent views on the causes, agents, and effects of globalization processes but they also comprise a number of internal disagreements even among its respective adherents. Held, McGrew, Goldblatt, and Perraton (1999) describe three schools of thought with respect to globalization as maintained by different groups in society. First, the "hyperglobalist perspective" holds that we have entered a new epoch in human history characterized by the dwindling importance and impact of nation states, and fueled by the economic logic of a global market. However, there is dispute among hyperglobalists as to what extent this is a positive evolution, i.e., whether the whole of humanity will be better off, or whether this will mainly create and reinforce inequalities. Proponents of the "skeptical perspective" tend to discard belief in the emergence of a global culture or governance structure and instead argue that we mainly witness more fragmented and regionalized situations, dominated by disguised versions of neoliberal economic strategies by the West, at the expense of large parts of the rest of the world. The "transformationalist perspective" takes into account a much wider range of factors and is consequently characterized by a more hesitant position with respect to the possible outcomes of globalization.

The term globalization is in fact a misleadingly simple concept to refer to a group of processes of tremendous complexity and magnitude. By the same token, the *antiglobalization* or *counterglobalization* movement, with its mission to reform unbridled forms of capitalism and competition, is somewhat misnomered, since it does not propagate cultural differentiation per se, nor nationalist or regional sentiments but rather a more supportive attitude toward all people and cultures as well as toward issues in need of a global solution (such as refugee crisis or climate change). Moreover, the term "anti-globalists" may host widely divergent criticisms of globalization (not just anti-corporate or anti-neoliberal globalization sentiments). So, by proclaiming to be "for" or "against" globalization without further qualification, one may find oneself in the unsought company of groups opposing globalization for quite different reasons (religious fundamentalists or extreme nationalist groups) (Stiglitz, 2003).

Globalization stands for "change" in many unpredictable ways and in many different domains. It should not be reduced to a one-dimensional process whereby local cultures are gradually supplanted by one dominant "world culture." As Steger (2014, p. 11) observes: "globalization is an uneven process, meaning that people living in various parts of the world are affected very differently by this gigantic transformation of social structures and cultural zones."

Cultural change and exchange are of all times and places, and thus the attempt to claim or maintain an "authentic version" of culture may in itself be a problematic position. Furthermore, local cultures and traditions are not necessarily less oppressive and more democratic. Globalization processes do not necessarily impede local cultures and at times may reinvigorate local cultures by creatively adapting or fiercely resisting the influx of new goods and ideas. Cultures in a globalizing world seem to have weakened (or transcended) their former geographical ties (for a large part through global media technologies, trade, tourism, etc.), a process which Tomlinson (2007) refers to as "de-territorialization." This alone already makes the study of cultures and cultural change more complex and demanding.

The focus on cultural aspects of globalization should, however, not obfuscate the fact that below the surface of the visually observable and the verbal rhetoric, which often takes the moral high ground, and behind a strongly propagated belief in technology as a prime driver of progress for all, there often lies a project of power expansion and recolonization (McMichael, 2017). Authors like Rosière and Jones (2012, p. 229) therefore challenge the dominant rhetoric of globalization by drawing attention to the fact that only some types of goods and services and some categories of people (wealthy travelers and businesspeople) are allowed to roam freely, while major parts of the world are exempted from the "right to move."

The idea or myth of a "borderless world" as a result of globalization has been debunked by border studies and globalization scholars alike, while it still lingers in popular discourse and politics (Rosière & Jones, 2012, p. 217). The persistence of borders and processes of rebordering rather than debordering, however, do not annihilate the actuality of hyperconnectivity and (inter)dependencies for better or for worse, but force us to rethink this complex phenomenon in relation to other processes and challenges. Counter to a widely held belief, Dubucquoy and Gaudot (2016, p. 40) emphasize that globalization has not necessarily weakened the state as a central pillar of the global system, nor has the state been supplanted by globalization.

The globalization idea also tends to relapse in times of mass migration and financial crises or pandemics. Nations are then inclined to fold back to their borders and to renegotiate their levels of solidarity. At such moments the praised

(mainly economic) interconnectivity often reveals serious supply chain vulnerabilities (e.g., shortage of medical equipment, oil, and food).

Yet, nationalism and protectionism are not the answers, and cross-border
solidarity and cooperation are needed more than ever to address the many global
challenges related to matters like climate change, health, migration, natural
resources, biodiversity, peace, distribution of wealth, equal opportunities, and
human rights.

3. MEASURING DIMENSIONS OF GLOBALIZATION: INDEXES AND RANKINGS

In an effort to make the elusive and multifaceted concept of globalization more
tangible and measurable, different instruments have been developed, usually in
the form of indexes. These indexes mainly result in rankings of individual cities as
well as whole countries with respect to their supposed level of globalization
(Dreher, Gaston, & Martens, 2008; Lockwood & Redoano, 2005). Most
globalization-related indexes are constructed around what are considered the key
dimensions of globalization: the political, the social, the economic, and their
various links with the technological. Behind those lists and scores are "indicators"
of sorts – with a varying degree of validity – which are often not known in detail
even to people who tend to ascribe value to them.

The urbanized world is clearly fascinated by rankings, lists, and awards: the
most livable city, the smartest city, etc. As Speed (2014) observes: "the gold
standard of city rankings is to become 'a world city,'" a sought-after title which is
acquired by ranking highly on various measures of "interconnectedness" with the
rest of the world. The list of the "World According to GaWC 2018 [Globalization
and World Cities research network]" (GaWC, 2020, see: https://www.lboro.ac.uk/
gawc/world2018t.html), for example, ranks cities according to their total scores
on a number of globalization parameters: the highest category of "Alpha++"
cities includes only London and New York, the "Alpha+" category comprises
Hong Kong, Beijing, Singapore, Shanghai, Sydney, Paris, Dubai, and Tokyo,
and then much longer lists of cities follow, respectively, under the "Alpha,"
"Alpha−" "Beta+" "Beta," "Beta−" "Gamma+" "Gamma," and "Gamma−"
categories. In a similar vein, Kaika (2017, p. 89) is critical of the call for "safe,
resilient, sustainable, and inclusive cities," which in her view "remains
path-dependent on old methodological tools (e.g., indicators), techno-managerial
solutions (e.g., smart cities), and institutional frameworks of an ecological
modernization paradigm that did not work." While urban scholars and social
scientists may be very critical about the provenance and the value of these
indicators, they often play an important role in political discourse.

Current indexes of globalization such as the KOF Index (Swiss Economic
Institute), the AT Kearney (2017) Index, the Foreign Policy Index, and the
CSGR Globalization Index (University of Warwick) try to measure the level of
globalization by a rather restricted – and sometimes even arbitrarily chosen –
number of economic, social, and political indices and variables (e.g., foreign

investments, trade restrictions, international tourism, internet use, foreign population, number of McDonald's restaurants, number of embassies, international treaties, etc.) (Dreher et al., 2008: see Fig. 1).

2019 Globalisation Index: Structure, variables and weights

Globalisation Index, de facto	Weights	Globalisation Index, de jure	Weights
Economic Globalisation, de facto	*33.3*	*Economic Globalisation, de jure*	*33.3*
Trade Globalisation, de facto	*50.0*	*Trade Globalisation, de jure*	*50.0*
Trade in goods	38.5	Trade regulations	25.8
Trade in services	45.1	Trade taxes	25.3
Trade partner diversity	16.4	Tariffs	25.4
		Trade agreements	23.5
Financial Globalisation, de facto	*50.0*	*Financial Globalisation, de jure*	*50.0*
Foreign direct investment	27.3	Investment restrictions	32.2
Portfolio investment	16.9	Capital account openness	38.7
International debt	25.7	International Investment Agreements	29.1
International reserves	3.2		
International income payments	26.9		
Social Globalisation, de facto	**33.3**	**Social Globalisation, de jure**	**33.3**
Interpersonal Globalisation, de facto	*33.3*	*Interpersonal Globalisation, de jure*	*33.3*
International voice traffic	20.0	Telephone subscriptions	40.6
Transfers	21.8	Freedom to visit	32.4
International tourism	21.2	International airports	27.0
International students	20.4		
Migration	16.6		
Informational Globalisation, de facto	*33.3*	*Informational Globalisation, de jure*	*33.3*
Used internet bandwidth	43.2	Television access	35.7
International patents	23.6	Internet access	42.0
High technology exports	33.2	Press freedom	22.3
Cultural Globalisation, de facto	*33.3*	*Cultural Globalisation, de jure*	*33.3*
Trade in cultural goods	28.0	Gender parity	26.2
Trade in personal services	24.3	Human capital	41.2
International trademarks	11.1	Civil liberties	32.6
McDonald's restaurant	20.9		
IKEA stores	15.7		
Political Globalisation, de facto	**33.3**	**Political Globalisation, de jure**	**33.3**
Embassies	36.2	International organisations	36.0
UN peace keeping missions	26.1	International treaties	33.6
International NGOs	37.7	Treaty partner diversity	30.4

Notes: Weights in percent for the year 2017. Weights for the individual variables are time variant.
Overall indices for each aggregation level are calculated by the average of the respective de facto and de jure indices.

Fig. 1. The Third Version of the KOF Globalization Index. *Source:* Gygli, Haelg, Potrafke, and Sturm (2019): Creative commons: http://creativecommons.org/ licenses/by/4.0/. The KOF Index of Globalization was first introduced in 2002 (Dreher, 2006) and subsequently updated by Dreher et al. (2008) and Gygli et al. (2019). The index intends to measure the economic, social, and political dimensions of globalization through quantifiable and weighted indicators. At some point, the number of IKEA (per capita) has been added as an indicator to complement the number of McDonald's restaurants in response to the critique that globalization was primarily thought of as a process of Americanization, but the index still embodies a primarily Western perspective. The most recent update of the KOF Index (version three) by Gygli et al. (2019) introduced a useful distinction between "de facto" (actual flows and activities) and "de jure" (policies and conditions) aspects of globalization, increased the number of variables from 23 to 43, and also added three variables in the domain of cultural globalization: "trade in cultural goods, trademark applications of non-residents, and trade in personal, cultural, and recreational services" (Gygli et al., 2019, p. 553). Note how even the "social" and "cultural" indicators are in fact very "economic" in nature.

The "Urban Elite Global Cities Index" – a collaboration of A. T. Kearney (management consulting), Foreign Policy (magazine), and the Chicago Council on Global Affairs – proposes a ranking based on five weighted dimensions of globalization: business activity (30%), human capital (30%), information exchange (15%), cultural experience (15%), and political engagement (10%) (Fig. 2). It is worth noting that "cultural experience" accounts only for 15% and is narrowly defined to include:

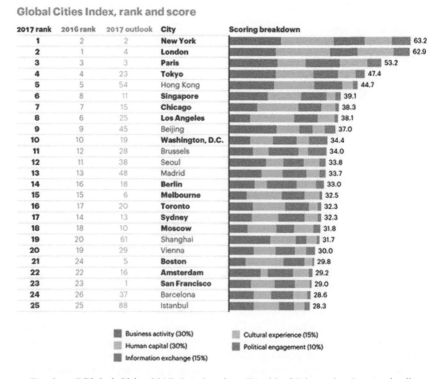

Fig. 2. "Global Cities 2017: Leaders in a World of Disruptive Innovation". Copyright A. T. Kearney, 2017. All rights reserved. Used with permission.

museums, visual and performing arts, major sporting events, international travelers, diverse culinary establishments, and sister city relationships.

Though the ambition to become a "global" city or a "smart" city (or both) is on the agenda of many politicians, institutions, and industries, to what extent this is a desirable status and for whom exactly is still up for debate. A "truly global city" as defined by the management consulting firm A. T. Kearney (in 2020 renamed to "Kearney") is "measured by its ability to attract and retain global capital, people, and ideas, as well as sustain that performance in the long term" (A. T. Kearney, 2017, p. 1). It is clear that such a vision embodies a particular kind of globalization from the perspective of an economic elite. Moreover, the KOF Index implicitly supports a particular form (aspect or version) of globalization (mainly understood as "Westernization") as non-Western globalizing trends are not measured (e.g., Islamic – or more broadly religious – forms of globalization and non-Western industries) (Potrafke, 2015, pp. 509–552). A. T. Kearney even proposes the concept of a "perfect" city, constructed from attributes of different high performing cities. Similar highly normative exercises fuel today's debate about what constitutes a "smart city." This raises the question of "smart" in what sense, for whom, and at what cost?

New indexes continue to be developed and current ones are being further refined. The "GlobalIndex," for example, which is firmly rooted in preexisting approaches to measure globalization, tries to provide additional noneconomic dimensions and indicators "encompassing interpersonal as well as aggregated economic, (socio)technological, cultural, and political relations" (Raab et al., 2008, p. 597).

Yet, most indexes seem to struggle with finding valid and robust indicators for the cultural dimension of globalization (Goodwin, 2020), and retain a primarily economic inclination. The cultural dimension indeed may be more difficult to measure than the economic, since "culture" (broadly defined) is in fact a dimension that encompasses most other dimensions and more. Completely missing in most indexes (except for the "Maastricht Globalisation Index," which is not discussed here) is an ecological dimension (Caselli, 2013, p. 2).

Important to note is that most indexes still use either nation state or city as their unit of analysis. Yet, countries or cities are not made up of homogeneous groups of people; rather they consist of individuals and groups that are affected in a variety of ways by different aspects and (side-)effects of globalization.

Caselli (2013, p. 5) therefore argues for a "plurality of perspectives" when trying to measure globalization, which should involve a "simultaneous use of tools based on different units of analysis." To that aim he proposes a Person-Based Globalization Index (PBGI) as a complementary perspective or tool, which would consider among other dimensions: the possession of resources, the effective mobility of individuals, and their participation in global flows.

A more visual approach may in fact contribute to a more pluralistic perspective by combining elements of nation states and cities, and above all by bringing the tangible effects of globalization on real people in everyday situations more to the fore. Some items of the existing indexes (e.g., the KOF Index, see Fig. 3) refer to phenomena that are to some extent visually observable in the urban context (e.g.,

2017 KOF Index of Globalization*

	country	Globalization Index		country	Economic Globalization		country	Social Globalization		country	Political Globalization
1.	Netherlands	92.84	1.	Singapore	97.77	1.	Singapore	91.61	1.	France	97.29
2.	Ireland	92.15	2.	Ireland	94.65	2.	Switzerland	91.13	2.	Italy	97.25
3.	Belgium	91.75	3.	Luxembourg	94.06	3.	Ireland	90.99	3.	Belgium	95.79
4.	Austria	90.05	4.	Netherlands	93.06	4.	Netherlands	90.71	4.	Sweden	95.56
5.	Switzerland	88.79	5.	Malta	91.74	5.	Austria	90.62	5.	Netherlands	95.41
6.	Denmark	88.37	6.	Belgium	90.08	6.	Belgium	90.34	6.	Spain	95.23
7.	Sweden	87.96	7.	Hungary	88.75	7.	Puerto Rico	89.98	7.	Austria	95.15
8.	United Kingdom	87.26	8.	United Arab Emirates	88.06	8.	Canada	89.22	8.	United Kingdom	94.67
9.	France	87.19	9.	Mauritius	88.01	9.	Denmark	87.54	9.	Brazil	94.30
10.	Hungary	86.55	10.	Estonia	87.54	10.	Cyprus	87.17	10.	Switzerland	93.40
11.	Canada	86.51	11.	Bahrain	87.37	11.	France	87.11	11.	Denmark	92.84
12.	Finland	86.30	12.	Slovak Republic	87.00	12.	Norway	86.31	12.	Norway	92.74
13.	Portugal	85.64	13.	Czech Republic	86.90	13.	United Kingdom	85.83	13.	Argentina	92.61
14.	Cyprus	85.00	14.	Cyprus	86.64	14.	Germany	85.49	14.	Egypt, Arab Rep.	92.46
15.	Czech Republic	84.88	15.	Denmark	85.76	15.	Croatia	85.29	15.	Canada	92.45
16.	Germany	84.57	16.	Austria	85.50	16.	Sweden	84.66	16.	Finland	92.34
17.	Spain	84.56	17.	Sweden	85.48	17.	Australia	84.13	17.	Turkey	91.88
18.	Slovak Republic	84.36	18.	Finland	84.20	18.	Finland	83.81	18.	Germany	91.71
19.	Luxembourg	84.21	19.	Georgia	83.01	19.	Portugal	83.39	19.	United States	91.43
20.	Singapore	83.64	20.	United Kingdom	82.99	20.	Spain	83.38	20.	Russian Federation	91.34
21.	Norway	83.50	21.	Latvia	82.80	21.	Slovak Republic	82.76	21.	Greece	91.33
22.	Australia	82.97	22.	Switzerland	82.76	22.	Czech Republic	82.19	22.	India	91.23
23.	Italy	82.19	23.	Portugal	82.71	23.	Hungary	81.16	23.	Hungary	90.94
24.	Croatia	81.39	24.	Montenegro	81.79	24.	Greece	80.74	24.	Nigeria	90.79
25.	Poland	81.32	25.	Qatar	81.45	25.	Lithuania	80.72	25.	Ireland	90.47
26.	Greece	80.60	26.	Seychelles	81.22	26.	Qatar	80.05	26.	Portugal	90.24
27.	United States	79.73	27.	Oman	81.02	27.	Poland	79.82	27.	Australia	90.17
28.	Estonia	79.27	28.	New Zealand	80.97	28.	Luxembourg	79.39	28.	Romania	89.82
29.	Qatar	78.49	29.	Chile	80.18	29.	Italy	79.37	29.	Korea, Rep.	89.58
30.	New Zealand	78.29	30.	France	79.41	30.	United States	78.82	30.	Morocco	89.50
31.	Malaysia	78.14	31.	Canada	79.08	31.	United Arab Emirates	77.93	31.	Chile	89.01
32.	Lithuania	77.47	32.	Brunei Darussalam	78.66	32.	Andorra	77.30	32.	Senegal	88.97
33.	Slovenia	76.91	33.	Panama	78.25	33.	Kuwait	77.28	33.	Poland	88.82
34.	Bulgaria	76.89	34.	Germany	78.06	34.	Israel	77.12	34.	Japan	88.10
35.	Romania	76.51	35.	Malaysia	77.93	35.	Malta	76.59	35.	South Africa	88.04
36.	Malta	75.86	36.	Slovenia	77.89	36.	Saudi Arabia	76.24	36.	Pakistan	87.30
37.	United Arab Emirates	75.29	37.	Spain	77.50	37.	Malaysia	74.20	37.	Jordan	87.17
38.	Israel	72.88	38.	Bulgaria	77.18	38.	New Zealand	73.99	38.	Indonesia	86.83
39.	Japan	72.26	39.	Poland	77.06	39.	Estonia	73.81	39.	Peru	86.38

Fig. 3. 2017 KOF Index of Globalization: Countries' Indices and Variables Weights. The ranking of countries rather than individual cities provides a quite different view: The Netherlands, Ireland, and Belgium top the 2017 KOF list while on "The World According to GaCW 2018" list (not shown here) the city of Amsterdam only takes the 34th position, Dublin the 40th position, and Brussels the 25th position. On the A. T. Kearney Global Cities 2017 chart (see Fig. 2), Brussels ranks 11th, Amsterdam 22nd, and Dublin is absent.

population mix, tourism (people, facilities), multinational shopping chains, embassies, and imports), but many aspects and manifestations of globalization escape these rather crude operationalizations of such a very complex and multi-faceted phenomenon. Cities and their diverse populations definitely require an approach that is more rooted in the day-to-day experience of city dwellers of all walks of life and of different levels of prosperity.

4. QUANTITATIVE AND GEO-LOCATED DATA VISUALIZATIONS OF GLOBALIZATION

A first step toward a more visual approach of globalization involves *visualizations* of quantitative data. These can be simple histograms like Fig. 2 above (Global Cities Index) or more complex hybrids of iconic and symbolic information, combining geographical positions with quantitative data and relationships.

Globalization as a concept and a circumscribed empirical reality has given rise to a number of visual representations of the nature and impact of this multi-faceted phenomenon. However, most of these visualizations are still based on quantifiable aspects of an economic nature.

More "imaginative" attempts to grasp the nature and extent of globalization as a particular concept and phenomenon than words and numbers involve different, often very sophisticated visualizations of numeric and geographic data (see Figs. 4 and 5, and the many creative visualizations at the GaWC web site: http://www.lboro.ac.uk/gawc/). Such sophisticated visualizations help to elevate the study of this complex phenomenon to a higher level of observation and understanding but often obscure the many intermediate operations such as the implicit conceptualization of what is and is not considered an aspect of global-ization, the exact weighting of factors, the choice of indicators and their com-bination, and the validity of the measurement instruments etc.

It is clear that the visualization of nonvisual data or aspects of phenomena reveals thought-provoking spatial and relational patterns, such as where the most globalized cities are situated, where there are clusters of globalization as defined by the Alpha city algorithm, and which parts of the world are unserved.

Using data visualization is thus an important step toward adding a visual dimension to the study of globalization: it may help to provide a macro view and allows us to keep track of existing relations and emerging patterns. However, these visualizations are still mainly based on a limited set of quantitative data and algorithms. Returning to the initial argument of this chapter, one should acknowledge that beyond the quantitative and the spectacular "iconic" (e.g., stunning images of the landmarks of a city) lies the everyday experience of people within those urban contexts.

An 'in situ' visual approach to globalization may help to uncover the "real life" impact and the specific contexts of these processes at different locations; the same "scores" for different cities or countries on a particular parameter may, in fact, stand for very different realities. Such a more qualitative and fine-grained

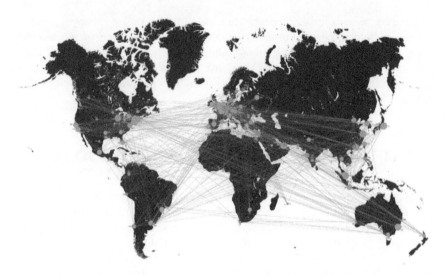

Fig. 4.   This Figure Shows Carta and González's Visualization of World
Cities and Their Interconnectedness, Based Upon the GaWC Data of 2010. The
Globalisation and World Cities Research network (GaWC), founded by the
geography department at Loughborough University, focuses primarily on researching
and charting the relations and transactions between cities, not just on the structure or
attributes of World cities as separate entities. The dots and their size locate the cities
on a geographic projection of the world, revealing the spread and importance of the
individual cities regarding their Alpha City status (top tier of world cities ranking).
But this chart goes further than simply locating cities on a map with an indication of
their globalization level as an individual attribute. The lines between the dots reveal
the interconnectedness between Alpha cities. © Crown copyright.

visual approach may complement and balance the dominant large-scale and
broad-brush quantitative approach.

5. METHODS AND TECHNOLOGIES FOR CAPTURING AND COMMUNICATING VISUAL ASPECTS AND EXPRESSIONS OF GLOBALIZATION

5.1 Visible Features and Markers of Globalization

While Steger's (2008) concept of a "global imaginary" does not refer primarily to
visual dimensions of globalization but to a widely shared consciousness of
belonging to a global community, the "visual" plays an important role in the
emergence of such feelings of interconnectedness (and in fostering or challenging
value systems in general), both through directly observable artifacts and behaviors and through mediated accounts (mainly, though not exclusively, of a
camera-based nature).

Fig. 5. To Address the Typical Setbacks of Large-Scale Network Data
Visualizations – Such as Visual Clutter and Unintelligible or Unappealing Form, and
Less Than Optimal Algorithms and Computing Power – Hennemann (2013, pp.
73–74) Developed this Circular Visualization (Based on 2010 GaCW Data of Office
Networks of Globalized Advanced Producer Services (APS) Firms, Such as Banks,
Insurance Companies and Consultancy Firms). This graphical representation, in
addition to mitigating the above-mentioned impediments, also attempts to introduce
an alternative way of including the geographical dimension (though with reduced
accuracy), which allows presentation of more informational attributes than the more
conventional two-dimensional representations.

Researching globalization "at street level" requires looking closely at many
layers and aspects of urban life. Numerous signs and symptoms can be found in
public spaces offering direct or indirect indications of the nature and experience
of different aspects of globalization. These need to be explored and identified as

potentially meaningful visible tokens ("visual indicators") of the meeting, merging, reaffirmation or resistance of (sub)cultures as they are set and enacted in everyday life. Such a more inductive and situated approach could add valuable insights to our knowledge and understanding of the complex and multifaceted nature of the phenomena that are grouped under the name globalization.

Studying human behavior in a public space (often particular hubs of inter-action: squares, parks, stations, and markets) mainly involves observing physical actions and expressions, as apparent in individuals and between individuals and groups of people sharing a space. Social behaviors are particularly interesting, and how cultural aspects have an impact on these activities. Observing and registering human behavior and the material impacts of that behavior (e.g., "erosion measures" and "tactical" alterations/interventions) may reveal the actual, changing, and amalgamated experience of partaking in a globalizing world.

The valid operationalization of particular concepts, processes and points of interest into concretely observable performances and artifacts as visual indicators is a crucial and demanding aspect, which will require a solid and varied knowl-edge base involving local experts of a variety of backgrounds. Any concrete study needs to clearly indicate what aspects of globalization are being looked at and how these can be approached (via indicators and appropriate methods to try to capture them). Researchers may, for example, be interested in: the impact of a more global context on the way sociability is enacted in public spaces, or how new technologies influence these behaviors as well as create new behaviors, or what elements of the visually observable environment indicate processes of hybridization, differentiation, and convergence, etc. Different observable marks of distinction with respect to class, religion, ethnicity, political or sexual prefer-ences and the whole realm of social (and a-social) behaviors like eating, sporting, talking, commuting, shopping, working, protesting, singing, dancing, arguing, fighting, looking, playing, and meditating may all be connected to particular aspects or dimensions of globalization processes.

5.2 A Concise Overview of Visual Methods and Resources to Study Globalization

The difficulties involved in investigating the "meeting" of cultures and the experience of living in a globalizing environment are for a sizable part method-ological in nature. City dwellers may rightfully be questioned about their views and experiences (through surveys or interviews), but the data gathered in this way do not always give a full and reliable view of what actually "happens" in these urban spaces, although they may offer important information on existing per-ceptions, and motivations, etc. Likewise, mere quantitative approaches offer a macro view based on aggregated data of only those aspects that can be quantified or are already available in numeric form.

Visual methods, with their focus on observable and unspoken aspects of society, have the capacity to uncover immaterial traits of society (norms, values, and expectations) by looking carefully at material artifacts as cultural expressions and at visual practices and performances of people.

A "street level" visual approach to globalization can productively make use of the broad variety of visual sources, methods, and techniques that have been utilized in and developed by visual social scientists (Pauwels, 2015; Pauwels & Mannay, 2020; Wagner, 1979). This rich array of methods ranges from collecting and analyzing existing or "found" visual data from a variety of sources, to the purposeful production of visual materials by the researcher in an exploratory, random, or systematic fashion, to using visual materials to elicit responses from respondents or to even ask respondents to produce visual materials in response to a research assignment. Finally, researchers may choose to use their visual materials and skills to communicate their findings and insights in novel, more experimental, and experiential ways like visual essays, interactive exhibitions, and the like.

5.2.1 Collecting and Analyzing Found Visual Materials

Visual media products depicting public spaces and human presence are being produced and made available at an increasing rate by a multitude of actors and for a variety of reasons. Numerous aspects of globalization are, therefore, invariably being visually documented and expressed – largely unintentionally – on a daily basis. So as a first visual mode of research into globalization, researchers may try to tap into this rich and varied offer of preexisting or "found" materials. This category of visual materials produced outside of an explicit research context is immensely broad and varied and so are the potential uses we can try to put them to. Each image source in this category provides the researcher with specific opportunities and problems in terms of what they can really reveal about the subject under study. Historic documentary images, maps, CCTV footage, satellite images, advertisements but also more private collections of family snaps or travel photography and artistic expressions like art photography, street photography, or feature films may be looked upon as documents of sorts with their own strengths and limitations, and thus require specific expertise to be used productively to study aspects of globalization. Of course, "found" materials may also include those visual materials that explicitly take globalization as a subject of critical commentary: cartoons (see Fig. 6), several recent documentary films, and images of protest against aspects or effects of globalization (see Fig. 7).

Found materials may contain useful synchronic (cross-cultural) or diachronic (historical) indications of processes of globalization, though researchers will have to make sure that they can acquire sufficient contextual information about these visual artifacts that originated outside their control. Yet, such "found" materials allow the study of events that predate a current research interest or that pertain to aspects of culture that otherwise would remain inaccessible for the researcher as an outsider. Some of these existing visual sources of information about the urban context in constant flux will be easily accessible (many web-based collections of individuals), while other sources will require difficult negotiations with respect to their access for research purposes and the way they can be used (e.g., surveillance camera footage and material from "official" sources in general).

Fig. 6. Cartoons Often Succeed in Highlighting or Condensing Aspects of Complex Processes and Ideas in Poignant and Funny Ways, Capable of Both Challenging and Feeding Stereotypes or Common Understandings. This cartoon uses the machine metaphor to challenge the devastating effects of free trade and globalization on the environment, natural resources, and workforce. *Source:* Rees (2019). Why place-based food systems? Food security in a chaotic world. Journal of Agriculture, Food Systems, and Community Development, 9(Suppl. 1), 5–13.

5.2.2 Researcher-Generated Visual Data Production

A more controlled and potentially more focused approach to studying globalization may include various types of *newly produced visual data by the researchers* (e.g., Figs. 8 and 9) *and their specialized collaborators.* Producing new visual data

Fig. 7. An Activist Expression Cunningly Utilizing the Iconography and Tag Line of a Leading American Soft Drink Brand to Warn us About an Imminent Global Threat. *Source:* Unknown.

Fig. 8. Researcher-Produced Image. A travel agency in Dubai: The Images (depicting visual icons of London and Paris) and the List of Destinations May Serve as Signifiers of a Particular Form of "Interconnectedness" of this Place with the Rest of the World. The displayed 50% discount for flights to and from Manilla targets the cheap labor force from the Philippines. *Source:* Photo by Luc Pauwels.

for answering specific research questions, however, poses limitations with respect to both time (the present) and space (physical and cultural accessibility). Visual data production strategies vary from exploratory and ad hoc recordings of events and artifacts by the researcher (to obtain a valuable first – but necessarily somewhat culturally biased – impression of the field under study), to more systematic recordings based on rigid sampling methods and using detailed *shooting scripts* (Suchar, 1997). Knowledgeable researchers walking the city attentively with a camera will indeed be able to quickly gauge essential dimensions and aspects of different globalization processes and effects, but these preliminary ideas often need to be further corroborated by more systematic observations.

For visually researching globalization in cities, it may suffice to record the data at one point in time per site ("time slice") or involve multiple recordings of the same spot or situation over time to gain a *diachronic or longitudinal perspective*. The first option may be suitable for synchronic research where, for example, the material culture of shopping areas in different cities are being compared at a certain point in time. When trying to record complex and volatile processes and situations, continuous recordings (film/video) or sequences of static images may be needed. *Interval photography* can be used for documenting changes in human behavior that occur at the same spot over a limited period of time (e.g., one image every 10 seconds or 10 minutes, depending on the nature of

Fig. 9. Researcher-Produced Image: Local and Global Icons Meet in the Center of Moscow in 2019. Brands and murals are among the most indicative markers of cultural change. While initially a token of interconnectedness, this image gains a much darker tone as a result of recent events. *Source:* Photo by Luc Pauwels.

the phenomenon one wants to capture). These images can then be placed next to one another for meticulous analysis. Another option, however, is to display them in rapid succession one after the other as a time-lapse movie, which allows the observation of flows and patterns of behavior (Pauwels, 2015). The term *repeat photography* (Rieger, 2011) is commonly used for projects that document slowly occurring changes, which thus require longer time spans between two recordings (e.g., several months, years, or decades); this implies that the image maker needs to return to same spot to seek the same framing and position. Interval recordings of microsocial behavior (e.g., interactions in a city square or in parks) may be very helpful to document, for example, culturally specific negotiations and expressions enacted while occupying and using particular spaces. Repeat photographs may prove particularly instrumental in documenting slowly occurring material and physical changes (see Figs. 10–15).

5.2.3 Participatory Visual Research: Actively Involving the Subjects of Globalization
Some methods of visual data production may also involve the subjects of globalization in more active ways and tap into their experience of a situation in a unique manner. For example, researchers could compile a set of visual stimuli (e.g., images of different cities with varying degrees of globalization, or images of

1980   1983

1986   1988

1993   2013

Figs. 10–15. Vyse Avenue at 178 Street, South Bronx, New York, 1980–1998. Camilo José Vergara's ongoing "Tracking Time" project is a unique collection of photographs, many of which exemplify the power of "repeat photography." In the introductory text of his website, Vergara clearly phrases the unique potential of his approach to document urban change: "For more than four decades, I have devoted myself to photographing and documenting the poorest and most segregated communities in urban America. I feel that a people's past, including their accomplishments, aspirations and failures, are reflected less in the faces of those who live in these neighborhoods than in the material, built environment in which they move and modify over time. Photography for me is a tool for continuously asking questions, for understanding the spirit of a place, and, as I have discovered over time, for loving and appreciating cities." *Source:* Photos by Camilo Vergara. https:// www.camilojosevergara.com/.

potentially problematic effects of globalization, or a set of images that depict the same urban spots over time, marking clear changes in material culture and inhabitants) and use this as a stimulus in a non-directive interview. This approach is known as *photo elicitation* (Collier & Collier, 1986), although in fact a more generic term like "visual elicitation" is preferable, since the visual stimuli may also be films or drawings, or other visual artifacts. The method generates often unpredictable reactions, factual information, and projective comments (triggered by elements in the images, rather than explicit questions by the interviewer) and helps to disclose the views and concerns of the respondents in a more sensitive and open-ended way than in traditional interviews.

However, research subjects may also be asked to produce visual materials in response to an assignment initiated or facilitated by a researcher – an approach called *respondent-generated image production* (RGIP: Pauwels, 2010) – and to comment on them afterward (see examples in Figs. 16 and 17). A selection of culturally diverse individuals living in the same city might, for example, be asked to make images of places and things that make them feel at home or comfortable, and also images of what they see as problematic or disconcerting. These visual testimonies or statements of how different individuals experience and view the globalizing urban context usually need verbal elucidation by their producers to explain the "why" of certain depictions but also will contain information that transcends the conscious intentions of their makers. The researcher scrutinizing the visual outcomes of such assignments in combination with respondent comments may yield unique insights into the personal and cultural experience of the respondent, both through what they include and what they leave out of the (static or moving) pictures and through study of the formal choices of the images (e.g., framing and camera distance). Respondent-generated images should not be confused with user-generated (visual) content (e.g., visuals that are spontaneously shared on social media); such content is being produced *outside* a specific research context or community project. Respondent-generated image production not only comprises the use of camera-based images, depicting aspects of the respondent's material world, but also includes a variety of drawing methods and techniques whereby the respondent or participant may be prompted to give a concrete shape to more internal processes and views or events of the past.

Whereas the purpose of respondent-generated image production in a research project is primarily to acquire unique data about the respondents' world (their visualized experiences and environment as an entry point to their culture) and thus to generate scientific knowledge, the primary aim of more activist versions of this method, often indicated with terms such as "photovoice" (Wang, 1999) and "community or collaborative video" (Mitchell & de Lange, 2011), is to initiate a positive change in the world of the participants, ideally by raising awareness of a problem in a community, by empowering community members or marginalized individuals, or by trying to exert influence on authorities or policymakers to improve a problematic situation. In particular, the problematic aspects of some emanations of globalization as well as their effects on local communities have been the subject of many activist participatory projects: see, e.g., PhotoVoice, (https://photovoice.org/), an organization "that designs and delivers tailor-made

Figs. 16 and 17. Examples of Respondent-Generated Image Production. Students in my visual studies seminar were asked to depict or express with photographs what the term "borders" meant to them. Sarah Tanghe depicted her parents (top) who became pen pals in their teens and surmounted different types of boundaries to create a happy family. A second photograph (bottom) by Sarah depicts a commemorative plaque and picture at a spot where a young man fell into the water and drowned: the ultimate border between life and death. *Source:* Photos by Sarah Tanghe.

participatory photography, digital storytelling, and self-advocacy projects for socially excluded groups," or Empowering the Spirit (http://empoweringthespirit.ca/), which promotes and exemplifies photovoice as "a participatory action research method that employs photography and group dialogue as a means for marginalized individuals to deepen their understanding of a community issue or concern."

5.2.4 *Analyzing Visual Data*

When analyzing and interpreting collected and newly generated visual data (as indexes, symbols, icons, and symptoms of culture), both visual and spatial semiotics (Krase & Shortell, 2011) can play a crucial role but other theoretical and analytical frameworks (e.g., iconology, rhetoric, discourse analysis, material culture studies, linguistic landscape research, etc.) can also be brought into play to allow differentiated readings of the visual environment. Such analysis is often steered by a validated set of "visual indicators" that were constructed with a grounded theory approach, while also more "holistic," syntagmatic readings can be performed on the data.

The visual analysis of nonverbal behavior as captured by visual media can benefit from different domains of study such as *proxemics*, which is the study of social and personal space as a "specialized elaboration of culture" (Hall, 1966, p. 1). This is an important theoretical framework with which to examine the spatial dimension of nonverbal behaviors of people in urban (indoor and outdoor) settings, but it is also suited to interrogate the physical design of space in houses, buildings, and cities as a whole. Other potentially useful theoretical approaches to the study of human behavior are *chronometrics* (the study of how time is structured and experienced differently by different people and cultures), "kinesics" (the study of facial expressions, gestures, and body movements; Birdwhistell, 1970), choreometrics (study of movement and dance; Lomax, 1975), and haptics (the study of interactions involving the sense of touch, though only partly visible; DeVito, Guerrero, & Hecht, 1999).

The primary purpose of a social scientific visual analysis is to discover significant patterns in the depicted (the "what") and in the manner of depiction (the "how"), to subsequently develop plausible interpretations that link observations to past or current social processes and normative structures. Visual analysis thus, in general, concerns the study of observable elements in the image or visual representation: people, attributes, physical circumstances, their organization, and multiple interrelations, but it should also include the study of the formal qualities of the visual artifact as a source of information about the culture of the producer. Although the depicted reality and its particular formal transformation often constitute the main focus of analysis, the broader context of the referent beyond the image frame should not be left unconsidered. Many elements within the image are but indications of aspects that are not directly visible or present within the frame: the broader culture within which the image originated, background information about the image producer and about the primary audiences and uses of the images, specific political, social, or physical circumstances etc.

5.2.5 Data Visualization and Conceptual Visual Representations in Visual Research

Visualizing quantitative data and using graphical representations of concepts or complex relations may both serve intermediate analytical steps and the final presentation and communication of insights and findings. Visual research approaches thus are not by nature uniquely qualitative. However, as has been made clear in the first part of this chapter, when discussing current indicators and visualizations of globalization, this complex phenomenon may benefit from a series of visual approaches that are focused on aspects that are visually observable in real life.

While the current hype around "big data" also seems to contribute to the idea that empirical research is becoming "more visual," one should be aware that this mainly pertains to making visible that which is not visual in nature (mainly visualization of quantitative data) and that it does not take advantage of the many visual dimensions of culture and society as a prime source of data. Moreover, it should be emphasized that visual research, which departs from visually observable data (e.g., people in public spaces), often resorts to counting and measuring particular aspects of a captured reality (densities, distances, and times), thus involving a transformative process to obtain more manageable quantitative data (which then again may be "visualized" in more abstract and conceptual ways). This should be done with the greatest care, as different types of visualizations invariably embody certain assumptions toward the referent (the subject of the depiction) and the subsequent uses of the visual representation.

5.3 Multimodal Communication of Visual Research on Globalization

The visual study of globalization is not limited to employing various data collection and production methods and techniques, but the visual dimension of this approach extends to the final presentation of the research, from using images and (quantitative) data visualizations in conventional articles, up to visual essays and fairly self-contained films (MacDougall, 2011; Pauwels, 2006) or multimedia products. Next to the reproductive and evidentiary ("mimetic") qualities of camera-based technologies, social scientists are gradually exploring the predicative or metaphoric ("expressive") qualities of the (photographic) image and of other visual and multimodal elements in novel, more experimental, and experiential ways. The visual essay, anthropological and ethnographic film productions, as well as other arts-based formats and traditions (e.g., digital storytelling, exhibitions, performances, and multimedia installations) try to push the boundaries of what is gradually being accepted as "scholarly" output (Pauwels, 2012).

Today the term "visual essay" is used for a variety of formats which have moved far beyond the paper-based pictures and text combinations or linear short movies. Boosted by new media technologies and networking opportunities, the visual essay has developed into a contemporary vehicle for voicing and visualizing all sorts of personal reflections, new ideas, arguments, experiences, and observations. It may take the form of a manifesto, a critical review, a testimony, a compelling story, or any possible variation and combination of these formats.

Expressive formats such as the visual essay and social scientific film require a judicious integration of distinct competencies relating to highly diverse domains.

Whereas some of the previously discussed forms of camera-based research can suffice with limited knowledge and skills for producing visual records to the required level of detail in a standardized way, the more visual and multimodal expressive modes, such as the visual essay format and fully fledged social scientific films, require a far higher level of visual competency. Such visual expertise involves many aspects (technological, analytical, creative, semantic, etc.) and a multifaceted aptitude to constructively integrate these visual elements with other expressive systems (e.g., sound, music and written or spoken texts) and with the norms and expectations of the discipline.

Two multimodal examples toward scientific expression in the context of the study of globalization are provided by David Redmon and Luc Pauwels. David Redmon's film *Mardi Gras Made in China* (2005; Fig. 18) is a powerful visual

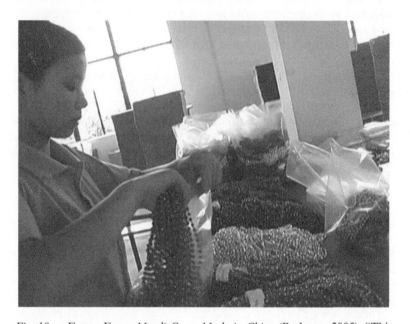

Fig. 18. Frame From *Mardi Gras: Made in China* (Redmon, 2005). "This examination of cultural and economic globalization follows the life-cycle of Mardi Gras beads from a small factory in Fuzhou, China, to Mardi Gras in New Orleans, and to art galleries in New York City." In the book, Redmon writes about this film (Redmon, 2015); the author explains that his purpose was to teach "readers to think critically about and question everyday objects that circulate around the globe: where do objects come from, how do they emerge, where do they end up, what are their properties, what assemblages do they form, and what are the consequences (both beneficial and harmful) of those properties on the environment and human bodies?" Both the book and the film are convincing illustrations of a "cultural biography approach" (Kopytoff, 1986) or as Redmon (2015) calls it "a commodity chain analysis," which follows the trajectory of an object to its origins. *Source:* Redmon (2005).

study of aspects of globalization as experienced and enacted by different groups of people and centered around the "cultural biography" of an object: Chinese workers produce beads that are used in New Orleans' Mardi Gras festivities. "Worlds of (In)difference: a visual essay on globalization and sustainability" by Luc Pauwels (2019; Figs. 19 and 20) then tries to express and problematize different aspects of globalization through purposefully made expressive

Figs. 19 and 20. Two Images Taken From "Worlds of (In)difference: A Visual Essay on Globalization and Sustainability". Fig. 19 epitomizes privileged spaces of global cities. A Rotterdam-based upmarket restaurant's name (The World) and tag line (All Day Meeting & Eating) on the shiny marble exterior inadvertently epitomize a "world of difference" in priorities between the social elites and the less fortunate in a globalizing world. *Source:* Pauwels (2019). Fig. 20 intends to link globalization with sustainability and biodiversity. The image made in Taipei seeks to communicate that much of nature may be on its way to the "exit" when not receiving truly global attention. The widely endorsed, but far from attained "goals for sustainable development" clearly summarize the main "global" challenges of humankind, which span almost all facets of life: the need to mitigate inequalities and imbalances in so many domains (wealth, gender, education, health, housing, power), the radical rethinking of dominant consumption patterns and current industrial and economic priorities, and the urgent need to take ecological issues and the preservation of natural resources more seriously. Metaphorical images such as these typically serve in more "expressive" scholarly products, when combined with an evocative text grounded in an academic body of knowledge. Pauwels (2019).

photographs and deliberate juxtapositions of images (with an introductory text) to construct an implicit argumentation.

5.4 Expanding the Scope: Emerging Technologies and Multisensorial Challenges

Finally, it is important to reiterate that various emerging technologies, which co-construct and steer the present-day experience of living in globalizing cities (smartphones, surveillance cameras, action cameras, personal and public screens and sensors, GPS devices, Google Earth and Street View, drones, and smart glasses), can also be employed to study globalizing urban contexts and can yield valuable and new types of data within each of the distinguished methods (see Fig. 21). The urban context is being documented visually for so many different reasons by authorities, institutions, and organizations, but equally by tourists and locals (Instagram and Flickr) on a daily basis. In addition, researchers can actively intervene and attach visual and geolocative devices to static and moving objects, to respondents, and to themselves. Thus, the experience and use of a globalizing city by concrete persons are being documented in its crucial visual (or visualizable), spatial, and temporal dimensions.

Obviously, there are more senses than the visual involved in experiencing the globalizing environment, which also comprises of a variety of sounds, smells, haptic sensations, and their complex interplay. Visual researchers are increasingly aware that notwithstanding its central role in cognitive and communicative processes, the visual should not be studied in isolation. Consequently, they try to expand their approaches to include as much as possible the other senses and the many expressive modes that are involved. However, although one can experience the contributions of each of these senses in direct encounters (e.g., when walking in an urban environment), it is much harder to permanently capture them for further study. Even the most hybrid and advanced (multi)media still only succeed in addressing two out of our five senses (sight and hearing) and largely fail to directly record and transmit tactile, olfactory, or gustatory sensations (individuals

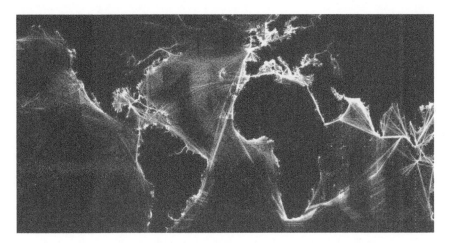

Fig. 21. A Visual Exploration of the Mostly Invisible Energy Shipping Routes Around the World Based on GPS Pings From Oil and Other Energy Carrying Vessels. As part of an interactive web platform, the data can be viewed across time, revealing changes in patterns of movement as the geopolitics, price of oil, and conditions at specific ports change. "Port to Port" by Juan Saldarriaga, Laura Kurgan, Dare Brawley, and Jen Lowe is just one of the many fascinating projects of Columbia University's "Center for Spatial Research" led by architecture professor, Laura Kurgan. This center focuses on the ethics and politics of new technologies of mapping, data visualization, data collection, and data analysis. It seeks to develop data literacy for different audiences in the era of big data to better understand the past, present, and future of cities worldwide (https://c4sr.columbia.edu).

can however try to note down and visualize these nonvisual and nonauditory experiences). What is technologically more feasible and brought into practice are measurements of bodily responses (heart rate, sweating, brain activity, and movements), while receiving sensory stimuli in real life or in experimental setups.

6. CONCLUSION: THE LIMITS AND PROSPECTS OF A VISUAL APPROACH TO GLOBALIZATION

This contribution examined the visual dimensions of globalization both as a directly observable and as a "mediated" field. Nonvisual empirical data on aspects of globalization can first of all be "visualized" in the sense of being transformed from symbolic (numbers) into more iconic and metaphoric form (visualizations) and thereby provide a better understanding of interrelations and trends as well as adding a spatial (often geographical) dimension to the data. However, one can also depart from visible elements of (urban) culture (artifacts and behavior) and instigate the production of visual records of those aspects for further scrutiny. Finally, a visual approach may not only document a phenomenon in rich detail (while inevitably a selective and reductive act) but also involve more metaphorical and constructive approaches that go beyond *depicting* the world but seeking to *reveal* a specific take on a phenomenon rather than simply depicting aspects of it. Such an "expressive," interpretative effort embodies the transition from mere data to the visual (multimodal) materialization of insight. While this chapter started by looking at existing visualizations of globalization, which are important as "found data," it should be clear that visualizations may also be produced by researchers to analyze their data (of a visual or nonvisual nature) and/or as researcher-produced end products to communicate their research in a partly visual manner.

A more visual approach to study globalization can also prove very rewarding in an educational context. Earnest and Fish (2014) vehemently promote the use of visual materials in the classroom to provide students with a basic understanding of the complex politics of globalization:

> Visual exemplars play an important role in both the study and the politics of globalization. Images diffuse international norms, reproduce prevailing assumptions, and inform our understanding of complex global processes such as financial crises, migration, and climate change. [. . .]. Visual material may express popular views about globalization, mobilize people to reform or resist its harmful processes, or reify existing assumptions about the bifurcation of the so-called First and Third Worlds. [. . .] Quite simply, imagery not only allows us to 'see' globalization, but also to observe how others envision it. (Earnest & Fish, 2014, p. 248)

Earnest and Fish (2014) further discuss distinct learning outcomes of using visual materials beyond an improved understanding of this phenomenon, including facilitating collaborative learning and active learning as well as allowing an affective dimension to enter the learning process, thus reframing "globalization from abstract and purely theoretical forms to tangible and personal encounters" (Earnest & Fish, 2014, pp. 250–251). Visuals prove invaluable for communicating messages on a global scale and thus for educating people outside the classroom (see Fig. 22).

Any instrument to measure globalization presupposes a specific conceptualization of what constitutes globalization, and as the phenomenon is so multifaceted, every measure is inevitably incomplete and biased. Therefore, a visual approach is not presented here as an all-encompassing alternative, but just as a complementary set of methods which is particularly suited (to a certain extent) to investigate the tangible impact of globalization.

While a visual approach to globalization may open new perspectives, in particular with respect to how this phenomenon and its many processes intersect with the experiences and appearances of everyday life, one needs to acknowledge its limitations. Visual observations and depictions of the physical world primarily reveal the "outer shell" of society: they provide very particularistic data, specific instantiations of particular processes in particular locales at particular times (and in that respect they are more truly empirical than some other types of data); they also provide more holistic types of interrelated data (elements in context), but for the most part, they remain just observable effects and symptoms which do not necessarily lay bare the multiple interacting and underlying causes.

Fig. 22. "Your Safety is My Safety." 'In situ' information board about a global threat. The recent COVID-19 pandemic highlighted the need to rethink and communicate the vulnerabilities and risks of a globalized world in its present shape, to develop controls and regulations to signal and mitigate the threats without leading to a complete reversal of the process of increased interconnectivity. Viruses, in particular, benefit from the exponentially increased mobility and connectivity of their hosts. Visuals play an important role in communicating these threats and how to handle them. *Source:* Photo by Luc Pauwels.

Material culture researchers and researchers skilled in spatial semiotics and local cultures, however, may be able to "decode" to some extent the signs and symptoms in the physical environment and succeed in relating observable cultural artifacts and human activities to the deeper, immaterial layers of culture, thus uncovering the realm of values, expectations, and aspirations.

With respect to analyzing human behavior in a public space, one can answer many important questions regarding who (age groups, subcultures, mixed or monocultural) uses particular places in a city and in what ways, and what kind of activities and interactions are taking place, etc. However, in particular with respect to behaviors that involve technological devices, one may see people "doing things" but distant observations do not always reveal exactly what they are doing (e.g., on their smartphone) or why. As Tomlinson (2007) rightly notes: "We have to be careful not to confuse mere cultural goods with the 'practice' of culture itself – which involves the interpretation and the appropriation of meanings in relation to such goods" (Tomlinson, 2007, pp. 356–357). So it does not suffice to simply record the presence of certain cultural goods and activities but one has to try to go deeper into how exactly these goods (e.g., smartphones, public screens, and signs) are being used in a particular social setting or culture and how they affect the deeper layers of culture. Visual research may provide various useful entry points to such a study, but often needs to be complemented by other methods, both established (surveys, interviews) and emerging ones (e.g., those monitoring online behavior).

Whether globalization is a useful concept for addressing contemporary processes of social and cultural change (or way too broad or limited to encompass a complex and hybrid of such magnitude) is subordinate to the observation that these phenomena of change and interconnectedness offer multiple visually observable entry points and unique opportunities for research. In other words, one does not have to buy into dominant notions of what globalization stands for or what constitutes a "global-" or "world city" to recognize the vast potential that resides in the thoughtful application of visual methods for researching cultural changes as spurred by flows of interconnectedness, nor to recognize the value of looking at the everyday reality of those rather abstracted, and sometimes obscurely quantified processes.

Visual approaches to globalization and cultural exchanges may help to enrich and complement the more abstract discourse of globalization and transnationalism (as well as those on "de-bordering" and "re-bordering") with empirically grounded and localized insights regarding concrete expressions and enactments of cultural encounters in urban settings. They may provide a more valid, unobtrusive way to assess and understand the impact of culture and cultural exchange on the daily life of inhabitants in cities around the world and add a unique "localized," cross-cultural empirical perspective to the many divergent views and discussions about the presumed beneficial or detrimental nature of these processes.

REFERENCES

Aiello, G. (2011). From wound to enclave: The visual-material performance of urban renewal in Bologna's Manifattura delle Arti. *Western Journal of Communication*, *75*(4), 341–366.

Birdwhistell, R. (1970). Kinesics and *context*. Philadelphia, PA: University of Pennsylvania Press.

Caselli, M. (2013, October–December). *Nation states, cities, and people: Alternative ways to measure globalization* (pp. 1–8). Los Angeles, CA: SAGE Open.

Collier, J., & Collier, M. (1986). *Visual anthropology: Photography as a research method* (Revised and expanded ed.). Albuquerque, NM: University of New Mexico Press.

DeVito, J., Guerrero, L., & Hecht, M. (1999). *The nonverbal communication reader: Classic and contemporary readings* (2nd ed.). Long Grove, IL: Waveland Press.

Dreher, A. (2006). Does globalization affect growth? Evidence from a new index of globalization. *Applied Economics*, *38*(10), 1091–1110.

Dreher, A., Gaston, N., & Martens, P. (2008). *Measuring globalization: Gauging its consequence*. New York, NY: Springer.

Dubucquoy, O., & Gaudot, E. (2016). 'The ocean: From colonised territory to global nation' in: Checkpoint Europe. The return of borders. *Green European Journal*, *3*(12), 35–43.

Earnest, D. C., & Fish, J. N. (2014). Visual sociology in the classroom: Using imagery to teach the politics of globalization. *Politics*, *34*(3), 248–262.

GaWC. (2020). *Globalization and world cities research network*. GaWC. Retrieved from http://www.lboro.ac.uk/gawc/

Gendelman, I., & Aiello, G. (2010). Faces of places: Façades as global communication in post-eastern bloc urban renewal. In A. Jaworski & C. Thurlow (Eds.), *Semiotic landscapes: Language, image, space* (pp. 256–273). London: Continuum.

Goodwin, A. L. (2020). Globalization, global mindsets and teacher education. *Action in Teacher Education, 42*(1), 6–18.

Gygli, S., Haelg, F., Potrafke, N., & Sturm, J. E. (2019). The KOF globalisation index – Revisited. *The Review of International Organizations, 14*(1), 543–574.

Hall, E. T. (1966). *The hidden dimension.* Garden City, NY: Doubleday.

Held, D., McGrew, A., Goldblatt, D., & Perraton, J. (1999). *Global transformations: Politics, economics and culture* (pp. 32–86). Stanford, CA: Stanford University Press.

Hennemann, S. (2013). Information-rich visualisation of dense geographical networks. *Journal of Maps, 9*(1), 68–75.

Huntington, S. P. (1993). The clash of civilizations? *Foreign Affairs, 72*(3), 22–49.

Kaika, M. (2017). 'Don't call me resilient again!': The new urban agenda as immunology ... or ... what happens when communities refuse to be vaccinated with 'smart cities' and indicators? *Environment and Urbanization, 29*(1), 89–102.

Kearney, A. T. (2017). *Global cities 2017.* Chicago, IL: Brochure.

Kopytoff, I. (1986). The cultural biography of things: Commodification as process. In A. Appadurai (Ed.), *The social life of things: Commodities in cultural perspective* (pp. 64–91). Cambridge: Cambridge UP. 1986 (reprint 2003).

Krase, J., & Shortell, T. (2011). On the spatial semiotics of vernacular landscapes in global cities. *Visual Communication, 10*(3), 367–400.

Lechner, F., & Boli, J. (2005). *World culture: Origins and consequences.* Malden/Oxford/VIC: Blackwell Publishing.

Lockwood, B., & Redoano, M. (2005). *The CSGR globalisation index: An introductory guide.* Centre for the Study of Globalisation and Regionalisation Working Paper 155/04.

Lomax, A. (1975). Audiovisual tools for the analysis of culture style. In P. Hockings (Ed.), *Principles of visual anthropology* (pp. 303–322). Den Haag/Paris: Mouton.

MacDougall, D. (2011). Anthropological filmmaking: An empirical art. In E. Margolis & L. Pauwels (Eds.), *SAGE handbook of visual research methods.* London/New Delhi: Sage Publications.

McMichael, P. (2017). *Development and social change. A global perspective* (6th ed.). Los Angeles, CA: SAGE Publications.

Mitchell, C., & de Lange, N. (2011). Community-based participatory video and social action in rural South Africa. In E. Margolis & L. Pauwels (Eds.), *SAGE handbook of visual research methods* (pp. 171–185). London/New Delhi: Sage Publications.

Nederveen Pieterse, J. (1996). Globalisation and culture: Three paradigms. *Economic and Political Weekly, 31*(23), 1389–1393.

Nederveen Pieterse, J. (2015). Globalization and *culture*: Global *mélange* (3rd revised ed.). Lanham, MD: Rowman & Littlefield.

Pauwels, L. (Ed.). (2006). *Visual cultures of science: Rethinking representational practices in knowledge building and science communication.* Lebanon, NH: University Press of New England.

Pauwels, L. (2010). Visual sociology reframed: An analytical synthesis and discussion of visual methods in social and cultural research. *Sociological Methods & Research, 38*(4), 545–581.

Pauwels, L. (2012). Conceptualizing the 'visual essay' as a way of generating and imparting sociological insight: Issues, formats and realizations. *Sociological Research Online, 17*(1), 1–11.

Pauwels, L. (2015). *Reframing visual social science: Towards a more visual sociology and anthropology.* Cambridge: Cambridge University Press.

Pauwels, L. (2019). Worlds of (in)difference: A visual essay on globalization and sustainability. *Visual Studies, 34*(1), 79–92.

Pauwels, L., & Mannay, D. (Eds.). (2020). *The SAGE handbook of visual research methods* (2nd ed.). Los Angeles, CA: SAGE Publications.

Potrafke, N. (2015). The evidence on globalization. *The World Economy, 38*(3), 509–552.

Raab, M., Ruland, M., Schönberger, B., Blossfeld, H.-P., Hofäcker, D., Buchholz, S., & Schmelzer, P. (2008). GlobalIndex. A sociological approach to globalization measurement. *International Sociology, 23*(4), 596–631.

Redmon, D. (2005). Mardi Gras: Made in China. Carnivalesque Films. USA, 71 min.

Redmon, D. (2015). *Beads, bodies, and trash: Public sex, global labor, and the disposability of Mardi Gras. Innovative ethnographies.* Abington: Routledge.

Rees, W. E. (2019). Why place-based food systems? Food security in a chaotic world. *Journal of Agriculture, Food Systems, and Community Development, Ithaca, 9*(Suppl. 1), 5–13.

Rieger, J. (2011). Rephotography for documenting social change. In E. Margolis & L. Pauwels (Eds.), *SAGE handbook of visual research methods* (pp. 132–149). London/New Delhi: Sage.

Ritzer, G. (2003). Rethinking globalization: Glocalization/grobalization and something/nothing. *Sociological Theory, 21*(3), 193–209.

Ritzer, G. (2009). The McDonaldization of *society*. Los Angeles, CA: Pine Forge Press.

Ritzer, G., & Atalay, Z. (Eds.). (2010). *Readings in globalization: Key concepts and major debates.* Hoboken, NJ: Wiley-Blackwell.

Robertson, R. (1995). Glocalization: Time-space and homogeneity-heterogeneity. In M. Featherstone, S. Lash, & R. Robertson (Eds.), *Global modernities* (pp. 25–44). London: Sage Publications.

Rosière, S., & Jones, R. (2012). Teichopolitics: Re-Considering globalisation through the role of walls and fences. *Geopolitics, 17*(1), 217–234.

Speed, B. (2014, August 29). What does this town have to due to become a "world city"? City Metric Retreived from http://www.citymetric.com/what-does-town-have-do-become-world-city

Steger, M. (2008). *The rise of the global imaginary: Political ideologies from the French revolution to the global war on terror.* New York, NY: Oxford University Press.

Steger, M. (2014). *Globalization: A very short introduction* (very short introductions series) (3rd ed.). New York, NY: Oxford University Press.

Stiglitz, J. (2003). *Globalization and its discontents.* New York, NY: W. W. Norton & Company.

Suchar, C. (1997). Grounding visual sociology research in shooting scripts. *Qualitative Research, 20*(1), 33–55.

Thornton, W. H. (2000). Mapping the 'glocal' village: The political limits of 'glocalization'. *Continuum: Journal of Media & Cultural Studies, 14*(1), 79–89.

Tomlinson, J. (2007). Cultural globalization. In G. Ritzer (Ed.), The Blackwell *companion to globalization* (pp. 352–367). Oxford: Blackwell.

Wagner, J. (Ed.). (1979). *Images of information: Still photography in the social sciences.* Beverly Hills/ London: Sage.

Wang, C. (1999). Photovoice: A participatory action research strategy applied to women's health. *Journal of Women's Health, 8*(2), 185–192.

Chapter 2

PERCEPTION IN MOTION – ALTERNATIVE RESEARCH TECHNIQUES FOR EXPLORING THE URBAN LANDSCAPE

Saskia I. de Wit

ABSTRACT

The urban environment is perceived through multiple senses in parallel, which means that visual understanding of space is aided and complemented by auditory, basic-orienting, and haptic stimuli – although mainly unconsciously. Sensory conditions are inherent attributes of urban places, but are often overlooked in research. To include these aspects in any way in analysis of the urban landscape, they need to be understood as properties of urban space, to be translated from attributes of the perceiver to attributes of the perceived. Using the relation between a designed garden and its suburban context in Bad Oeynhausen (DE) as an example, I will explore an alternative analytical methodology that takes the first-hand perspective view of the subject moving through the city as the starting point. The human body explores space by moving through it; walking is the most direct way to access, study, and research the physical qualities of the (urban) landscape, involving not only visual experience but also sound, rhythm, kinaesthesia, balance, and so forth. A notation technique that discloses the interrelation between visual qualities and their perception over time is the technique of 'scoring'. Scores are symbolisations of processes, which extend over time. They can objectively represent non-visual qualities of space, communicating the relation between such processes and their spatial context to others in other places and other moments. These representations of movement expose the qualities of the

Visual and Multimodal Urban Sociology, Part B
Research in Urban Sociology, Volume 18B, 39–61
Copyright © 2023 by Emerald Publishing Limited
ISSN: 1047-0042/doi:10.1108/S1047-00422023000018B002

surroundings that change as one moves through them, thus communicating the experiential aspects of urban landscape.

Keywords: Score; time-based analysis; multi-sensory urban landscape; narrative analytical methods; perception; Wasserkrater garden; Bad Oeynhausen

1. INTRODUCTION

... The greatest treasures and most admirable things are hidden underground, and not without reason. (Rabelais, around 1564, 5.47)

The Wasserkrater garden is a suburban garden. It is a garden in a suburban context, but it is also literally placed underground, beneath the urban field, reaching down underneath the ubiquitous urban landscape. The garden is situated in the suburban agglomeration which includes the towns of Bad Oeynhausen and Löhne, near Hanover (Germany). In the sunken garden an artificial crater is set, from which a forceful water jet ejects at irregular intervals. When approaching the garden, the noise of the fountain, the risk of getting wet, the effects of light and shadow and the earthy smell of the underground space become strongly present. The different stages of entrance – building up to the inescapable downward movement of the spiral staircases into the crater – form a series of thresholds, marking the transition from the horizontal suburban field to the vertical suburban space, literally under the city. The resulting focus on the sensorial qualities of this place draws the attention to the temporal, climatic and geographic specificity that determines each place as unique.

When studying the effect that urban conditions have on the everyday life of individuals and communities, it is instrumental to start with these specificities that determine the urban landscape. To extract meaning from what we can see around us, we first need to study what it is that we see around us. What is this physical environment that people perceive day in, day out, often without even realizing that they do? What is the perceivable form of the urban landscape that creates the conditions and the organisation of the sensory experience, the source of the meaningfulness individuals and communities derive from, or attribute to, where they are? As anthropologist David Howes claimed, such a renewed attention to the senses in urban studies is not 'simply another stream of theory to add to our academic repertoire of colonialism, gender, embodiment or material culture, for example. Instead, the senses in their supposed immediacy are the medium through which such aspects are accessed or experienced' (Paterson, 2009, pp. 774–775). Current urban discourse has plentiful justification for taking into account a range of perceptual sensibilities as informants for understanding and working with the urban landscape. However, this accounting is difficult because of the emphasis on visuality and visual metaphors in the Western culture. 'As opposed to the formal structures of cognition, the senses seem unreliable as [...] parameters' (Malnar & Vodvarka, 2004, p. x). They are ephemeral, taking place in a moment in time and require human presence, and are thus of a different order than visual information. Therefore, the many ephemeral and non-visual qualities of the environment that constitute its perceivable form receive little attention in research. Partly, this lack of attention is due to the limiting effect of traditional techniques for analysis. Traditional research methods fall short when addressing the multi-layered, diverse and ever-changing nature of the urban landscape. And that which cannot be drawn or measured tends to be overlooked. How to draw what cannot be seen? What alternative modes of knowledge production can be used?

In this chapter I will use the analysis of several sensorial conditions of the near surroundings of the Wasserkrater garden to explore an alternative analytical methodology of the urban landscape: a methodology to visually represent ephemeral aspects of the urban landscape. Its central component is the score, a technique that takes the first-hand perspective view of the subject moving through the city as the starting point for understanding the urban landscape, aiming to do justice to the multi-sensory and time-based qualities of the urban landscape, such as visual sequences, dynamics of spaces, locomotion, surface qualities and sound.

2. THE FORM OF THE URBAN LANDSCAPE AS A RESERVOIR OF MULTI-SENSORY EXPERIENCES

In Sophocles' tale of *Oedipus at Colonus*, the blind Oedipus is led by his daughter Antigone. When he asks where they are, she replies that where they now stand '... is surely sacred ground, where vines and laurels and olive trees grow wild; a haunt of birds, where nightingales make music in the coverts' (trans. 1975, p. 5). In the following conversation it becomes clear that although Antigone did not know the precise location, this combination of perceptual elements convinced her it was a divine and special place: a defined site with a spring or brook, tree grove, a flower meadow, birdsong, breeze and shade. In this place of delight smells, sounds, taste and touch play an important role alongside the visual aspect. In Greek as well as Roman literature a place with these characteristics would be immediately recognised as being divine or special. Landscape is understood here as abundance, and the perception of this fullness is multi-sensory, associated with qualities that do not belong to an eye-minded worldview, such as sound, smell and taste (De Wit, 2018, p. 403).

People relate to environments through all their senses. From the perspective of multi-sensory perception, landscape – both urban and non-urban – can be considered a reservoir of sensory possibilities, giving substance and shape to human relations and activities. The qualities of the urban landscape only become meaningful if they can be experienced. 'If there can be no form without meaning, there can be no meaning without form' wrote architect Steven Kent Peterson (1980, pp. 88–113), when discussing what constitutes the physical form of the contemporary city. The perceivable form of the urban landscape creates the conditions and the organisation of the sensory experience that is the source of the meanings/meaningfulness each of us derives from, or attributes to the environment. As Arnold Berleant (1997, pp. 2–18) noted, the interrelated and interdependent union of people and place is one of perceptual experience, which includes sensory elements, as well as memory, knowledge and the conditioning and habits of the body and affects the range as well as the character of any environment. Whether or not we are aware of the sounds or smells that surround us, or of the quality of the light, these are part of the human habitat and enter into our perceptual experience. As architecture theorist Malcolm Quantrill (1987, p. 46) brought forward, people are constantly filtering the sensory input they receive, translating input into information and constructing meaning. They read places through engaging all senses, sight as well as sound, smell, taste, balance and touch; knowledge of place is a fact of (sensory) perception. Through the sensuous relationship of body–mind–environment, multi-sensory perception creates an awareness of place.

In contemporary discourse on the human relationship to the urban environment in terms of embodied experiences and affective relationships (Hayden, 1995; Massey, 1993; and others), the emphasis in defining perception is on the reception of sensory stimuli (information seeking), as if what we perceive is a characteristic of the perceiving subject. However, as sociologist and political scientist Eugene Victor Walter wrote in *Placeways*, sensory information is in the first place an asset of the perceived object, place or landscape: 'A place is a location of experience. It evokes and organizes memories, images, feelings, sentiments, meanings, and the work of imagination. The feelings of a place are indeed the mental projections of individuals, but they come from collective experience and they do not happen anywhere else. They belong to the place' (1988, p. 21). Sensory conditions, the organisation of sensory experience, are inherent attributes of urban places. Thus, the main question is not whether or how inhabitants consciously perceive what is there to be perceived – the meaning we derive from the urban environment, as an asset of the perceiver – but to unearth what it is that the place holds – as an asset of the perceived: the perceivable form of the urban landscape.

3. PROXIMATE PERCEPTION

In order to study the different aspects of perceivable form, we need to know something about how we perceive. Sensory perception of the physical surroundings is not a collection of separate experiences, perceived through different senses, but takes place through interrelated sensory systems. Psychologist James Gibson (1966) distinguished the visual, the auditory, the taste–smell, the basic-orienting and the haptic system. The perception of the physical landscape is a complex facility where one employs modes of perception ranging from the more direct and passive senses of taste and smell, touch and sound to active visual perception, combined with the indirect mode of symbolisation, and visual and symbolic understanding of space is aided and complemented by auditory, basic-orienting and haptic stimuli. For example, the reflection of sound can provide information about size and form of spaces (acoustics), and the amount of sound to enter from the surroundings demonstrates the measure of enclosure of a space.

The relation between space and sensory perception is defined by distance. Each sensory system has a different reach, and a different focus; some senses are proximate, others distant. Aural cues do give a sense of distance, but sound presents a smaller world than what eyes can potentially see. In open space, sounds do not carry as far as light, and smell has an even narrower scope. Taste and touch can only be experienced upon direct bodily contact. Because weight, pressure and resistance are part of the habitual body experience, people unconsciously identify with these characteristics in the forms they see. In 1929, geographer Johannes Granö defined two realms of perception, the *Fernsicht* and the *Nahsicht* (Granö & Paassi, 1997). According to Granö, *Fernsicht* [distant view] is the part of our environment we mainly experience by vision: the landscape, determined by the horizon. *Nahsicht* [proximity] is the environment we can experience with all our senses. A distinction that Bernard Lassus (1998) described as a distinction between the tactile scale and the visual scale. Visual experience distances us from tactile experience, and it dematerialises the world. When objects are out of reach, they lose their tactility, and the world becomes a pure spectacle. Proximity on the other hand makes one attentive to the material reality of earth, pavement or walls, like mass, grain, fragility or suppleness.

Therefore, in order to perceive the material world, the tactile, or haptic qualities are central. The material reality is that which can be perceived by the haptic senses. The word 'haptic' stems from the Greek verb *haptein*, which can be translated by 'grasping', to lay hold of something: to touch, to cling, to fasten, to latch on to. It refers to the sense of touch, but it suggests a wider experience of clutching and holding that does not stop with the hands but involves the entire body, and includes temperature, pain, pressure and kinaesthesia (the body sensation and movement of the muscles, tendons and joints, as in walking, climbing, swinging or rocking). Thus, haptic perception is the active exploration of surfaces and objects, the result from how various sensibilities of the body respond to the body's position in the physical environment. The term evokes many different ways of contact, involvement and participation, which can be divided into two distinct faculties. It refers to pressure to the skin, or literally the contact between the body and its environment, and to kinaesthesis, the ability of the body to perceive its own motion. Haptic perception can be described as 'the way the whole body senses and feels the environment [including] our feelings of rhythm, of hard and soft edges, of huge and tiny elements, of openings and closures, and a myriad of landmarks and directions' (Bloomer & Moore, 1977, pp. 34–36). Haptic cues refer to both space and substance and provide a location and orientation in relation to the place we perceive. Since haptic perception is participatory, active and passive at the same time, it reminds us that we are not only observers of the world but also actors in it. Haptic perception is about both an awareness of presence and of locomotion – a combination of tactile and locomotive properties, engaging in feeling and doing simultaneously.

4. WALKING

The corporeal awareness of the presence of the observer in space in combination with the action/reaction characteristic of kinaesthetic experience – the sensation of movement – are primarily responsible for the understanding of three-dimensional space. The human body can explore space only by moving through it. As Gibson (1966) stated: 'Not only does [locomotion] depend on perception but perception depends on locomotion inasmuch as a moving point of observation is necessary for any adequate acquaintance with the environment. So we must perceive in order to move, but we must also move in order to perceive' (p. 223).

In 1970 the land artist Robert Smithson created *Spiral Jetty*, a spiral of rock and earth, reaching out from the shore of the Great Salt Lake in Utah, which, through its isolation, addresses aspects of nature, time and endless space (Fig. 1). The Spiral Jetty is hard to reach, and the intense awareness of space and time is gained by a combination of the visual image of the weird shimmering air above the pink lake, and the bodily sensation of attempting to keep or regain a foothold when negotiating the rocks of the partially submerged jetty, and the feeling of the crusts and algae underfoot that are accumulated during long alternations of low and high water levels. In the vast, desert-like landscape the natural forces are evident. This artwork seems a totally different project from the photo essay Smithson had created only three years earlier, *The Monuments of Passaic*, a photojournalistic documentation of moments such as a parking lot, a sandbox, the concrete abutments of a highway-in-progress, a pumping derrick partly supported by pontoons and a set of six pipes – which he viewed as a horizontal

Fig. 1.   The Spiral Jetty, by Robert Smithson (1970). The artwork can only be experienced by walking to and over it. Negotiating the irregular rocks, one experiences the effects of time and nature. *Source:* Photograph by Sebastiaan Kaal (2011).

fountain – that pumped water from a pond into the river (1967, pp. 48–51). The New Jersey city Passaic is a car-oriented suburban/industrial landscape, hardly accessible on foot. Instead of viewing the mosaic of urban fragments on the map or the blur of passing 'pictures' of the landscape that one would normally see when sweeping past in a car, Smithson chose to approach the urban landscape from the intimate vantage point of the pedestrian, physically immersing himself inside these 'pictures'. This allowed him to appreciate similar wilderness qualities in the 'gaps' in and between the suburban and industrial fragments of Passaic as in the natural landscape of the Great Salt Lake. The physical experience of walking along the virtually inaccessible banks of the Passaic River allowed him to literally enter a temporal and perceptual 'elsewhere'. Comparing these two artworks shows the value of the conscious act of walking to disclose qualities of the urban landscape that remain otherwise hidden. These sensory conditions can be seen as inherent attributes of the urban landscape, which serve as a stimulus or catalyst for the transaction between people and space.

Walking is the most direct way to perceive the (urban) landscape, which not only involves visual experience but also includes the perception of sound, rhythm, kinaesthesia, balance and so forth, a multi-sensory, active interaction with the urban landscape, rendering the landscape a structure of spaces seen as well as felt, touched and heard. In walking we move into a near-sphere of our own choosing, which puts an emphasis on the materiality and the perception thereof: haptic perception. Thus, when attempting to 'capture' the city, walking can be an excellent tool, an embodied way of knowing. As Mark Paterson elucidated: '"a tactile perception of space" is a good starting point for an embodied ethnography of walking, thinking of our embodied everyday stance not as the separation of mind from body, head from feet, but as diverse strands of sense returns from limbs, viscera, sense organs and muscular movement that variously combine as an almost elastic sensory-spatial envelope, a sensorium in action' (2009, p. 777).

Walking the urban landscape is the enfolding of a spatial sequence, like a narrative. The writer Rebecca Solnit (2001), author of *Wanderlust: A History of Walking*, explains 'Part of what makes roads, trails, and paths so unique as built structures is that they cannot be perceived as a whole all at once by a sedentary onlooker. They unfold in time as one travels along them, just as a story does as one listens or reads, and a hairpin turn is like a plot twist, a steep ascent a building of suspense to the view at the summit, a fork in the road an introduction of a new storyline, arrival the end of the story' (p. 201). When discussing the role of walking as an instrument to read landscape form, landscape historian John Dixon Hunt (2003) suggests the procession as 'a ritual movement that follows both a preordained path and purpose, which is, on account of its prescription, repeatable on innumerable occasions' (p. 188), posing that a subject moving through space needs the help of prescriptions laid down in formal records such as social or religious convention or written text. I would suggest on the contrary that it is (the haptic properties of) the physical landscape itself, not any type of formal record, which is the prescription. These properties provide the clues to the choreography of space; the messages of the theatrical staging of squares and streets, the steepness of slopes, steps, entrances and vistas provide the events for the narrative. But where a written narrative unfolds in time and the space for its action is merely suggested; in the urban landscape the organisation of space is real and is the property that suggests or generates the time dimension, by establishing a sequence of movement through it.

However, the act of walking is only the first step in an analytical methodology of drawing out the perceivable form of the urban landscape. To disclose the sensory conditions as physical information to be found in urban landscape, these conditions need to be linked to the formal/physical components of urban space, and they need to be translated from attributes of the perceiver to attributes of the perceived. This asks for these two interrelated actions: walking and notation.

5. SCORING

It is relevant to be aware of the limitations and influence of notation techniques. More than representations of analytical content, notation techniques determine the limits of the analysis. They control what happens, as Lawrence Halprin (1969) explained, and he recounted that when the American avant-garde composer John Cage was asked: 'When you compose do you think notation first or sound first?' he replied: 'Both constitute inseparable entities, I cannot separate them' (p. 11). Thus, in a methodology that has walking, kinaesthetic experience, at the basis, the accessory notation technique is inseparable from the specificities of moving along a line. Whereas traditional analytical drawing techniques for urban spatial analysis, such as mapping, have space at the basis, this unfolding in time entails that notation techniques that represent perception in motion need to have time at the basis.

In the 1960s and 1970s, urban planners such as Gordon Cullen, Edmund Bacon and Kevin Lynch devised alternative notation techniques for analysing and designing that took the eye-level perspective view and the multi-sensory and time-based experiences of the subject moving through the city as the starting point. As is the case today, 'classical', top-down steered analysis, design and planning instruments were put into question during this period, as a result of changing cultural, social and economic circumstances that called for a revision of the discipline (Havik, Notteboom, & de Wit, 2017, p. 3). Donald Appleyard, Kevin Lynch, and John Myer (1964) devised their own scoring techniques to analyse the experience of moving along the motorway in their seminal analysis *The View from the Road*. They drew sets of several sequence diagrams, each highlighting a specific property of the visual spatial experience related to movement in a car, to extract and compare the different aspects of visual-spatial experience: sense of motion and space, orientation, proportion and scale, light. Likewise, Gordon Cullen (1961) and Edmund Bacon (1974) created serial visions, or visual sequences, of the spatial-visual conditions of the urban landscape (Fig. 2). Contrary to common interpretation, it is significant to note that their drawings are not merely representations of visual impressions, but sequences of 'sensations' (in Bacon's words) or 'revelations' (in Cullen's), bearing witness of all kinds of human interaction with space, of periodic occupation and appropriation

Fig. 2. Serial Vision (Gordon Cullen, 1961). 'To walk from one end of the plan to another, at a uniform pace, will provide a sequence of revelations which are suggested in the serial drawings [...] The even progress of travel is illuminated by a series of sudden contrasts and so an impact is made on the eye'. (Gordon Cullen, The Concise Townscape, The Architectural Press, 1961, p. 17).

of space, and of social interaction informed by spatial characteristics. These serial visions are registrations of the visual-spatial aspects of the landscape that are disclosed by locomotion.

However, to consider the multi-sensory aspects of the physical surroundings we need to expand the possibilities of these time-based registrations. In the same period as the above-mentioned group of urban planners, the American landscape architect Lawrence Halprin attempted to find a notation technique to include experience and perception in spatial design. Halprin's wife Anna was a chore-ographer and inspired by the close relationship Halprin thus had to dance and theatre, the choreography of movement became a key notion in his designs. In the 1960s he invented a personalised ideographic system, using 'scores' to choreo-graph the movement of elements in urban parks, plazas and cultural centres (Fig. 3). Derived from the traditional musical score, scores are symbolisations of processes, which extend over time. Halprin (1969) devised scores for all fields of human endeavour, such as street scores, ecological scores, city scores and com-munity scores. Communicating processes over time and space to others in other places and other moments, such scores can indeed objectively represent non-visual qualities of space. The essential difference with classical analytical drawings is that time, rather than space, is the framework. Halprin invented the word 'motation' for the particular type of score that represents motion, move-ment in space.

Whereas Halprin's scores took the actor as the subject (similar to the scores used in dance and theatre), as a research tool they can be pushed further by taking the physical landscape as the subject: a shift from how people act and perceive in space to how space and place can determine action and perception. In this way scores can be employed to register various aspects of a route, to objectify personal experience as the basis for site analysis. By dissecting experiences during and after walking different routes, several modes of perception can be translated into diagrams to express, for example, turns in the road, ascents and descents, road crossings, as well as spatial proportions, sound and vision. In order to grasp the relations between the several perceptual properties, these diagrams can be synchronised by drawing them as diagrams of a stretched surface section, with a horizontal axis representing the distance (which is the unifying factor), and a vertical axis representing the change in perceptual quality.

6. DIFFERENT SENSORY COMPONENTS

Let us take a closer look at the example we started with, to explore different possibilities for analysing the sensory qualities of the urban environment. The medium-sized town Bad Oeynhausen in Germany is part of an expansive sub-urban agglomeration (Fig. 4). In the centre of town a large fountain taps into the underground water source, as a reference to the town's origins as a spa town. From this fountain, the Jordansprudel, we walk to Park Aqua Magica (Agence Ter), created in 1997 to give an impulse to region and reconnect to the thermal history. At the centre of the park is the Wasserkrater garden, a sunken space

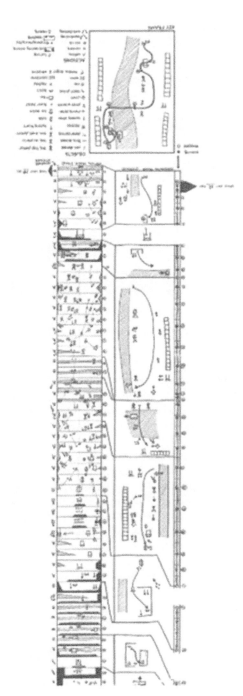

Fig. 3. Motation Score of Nicollet Mall Between Sixth and Seventh Street. For his conversion of Nicollet Mall, Minneapolis' main shopping street, into a pedestrian space, Halprin observed and analysed how people moved through space (Lawrence Halprin, 1969). *Source:* © Lawrence Halprin Collection, Architectural Archives, University of Pennsylvania.

Fig. 4.   The Suburban Landscape of Bad Oeynhausen. *Source:* Photograph by
Sebastiaan Kaal (2012).

around a large water jet that erupts at irregular intervals, created to expose the
invisible underground water landscape (Fig. 5). The route is a collection of
existing and new roads, paths, stairs and bridges, a sequence of events, with the
beginning and the end emphasised by the two fountains. Walking from fountain
to fountain would take at a leisurely pace 10–15 minutes.

To unravel the information that can be gathered on such a walk, I visited Bad
Oeynhausen on several occasions and in different weather conditions, each visit
making the walk from the Jordansprudel to the Wasserkrater. Walks like this are
best conducted in pairs, so each change in visual cues, sounds and body equi-
librium can be noted, voiced and discussed. During the walk, maps were used to
annotate the location and quality of each change, and photographs were taken to
document them. Later, these notes were translated into scores, with the aid of
cartographic information to objectively document locomotive aspects.

The most straightforward is a traditional score such as the ones created by
Cullen and Bacon: the visual score. As an analytical tool they go beyond regis-
tration, they are informed interpretations, singling out those spatial cues, which
are crucial for the scenography of the routing: composition elements that direct
the line of movement: landmarks, incidents, thresholds and gates. The vertical jet
of the Jordansprudel forms an explicit landmark. Next, a bridge over the forested
railway ravine provides a view into the far distance of the train lines. The path
continues through a natural valley, and a gabion wall points to a simple set of

Fig. 5.   The Wasserkrater Garden, With the Central Steel Crater Viewed
From the Sunken Space of the Surrounding Garden. *Source:* Photograph Sebastiaan
Kaal (2012).

stairs, out of the valley into the park. The wall is the first of a series of gabion
walls that brings coherence and direction. In the park the route becomes more
obvious, ending with a view out over the open agricultural landscape. Among
several circular plantations, one that seems but a low clump of shrubs subtly
marks the position of the Wasserkrater garden. At times the erupting jet of water
attracts the attention and indicates there is more to it than a clump of shrubs. The
clump turns out to contain a sunken garden planted with serviceberries (*Ame-
lanchier lamarckii*), and the depth of the garden is such that the canopy reaches
the level of the upper edge, reproducing the horizon of the terrain. The jet directs
the visitor away from the path to a ramp that leads down into the garden, making
it the inevitable culmination of the routing. From the moment of entering the
garden, the visual fields are shifting. Viewed from the park the garden was
obscured by the treetops below eye level, directing a horizontal view, but upon
entering the garden the view is directed downwards, as one can only do when
descending. In the garden the tree canopy creates a low ceiling and again directs
the view horizontally. Once inside the sunken garden, the visitors find their way
over a scattering of stepping stones in a carpet of plants, to one of the two narrow
slits with heavy doors in a steel circular wall. Here, a platform like a balcony
offers a view to the space below. The crater directs the view downward, into the
earth, and the eyes are drawn to the spectacle of the fountain below. Upon
entering, steep spiral stairs lead down to the bottom of the crater, where the

fountain directs the eyes upward to the sky. The defined space creates a connection to the natural space – both above and below ground – in the field of undefined and fragmented space of the suburban landscape (Fig. 6).

Much of the spatial-visual information that is perceived by the different faculties of the human body transcends what can be represented in perspectival images, the information that addresses the haptic component of spatial dynamics: the sequence of shapes, dimensions, proportions, arrangements and depth of volumes, textures, flexibility and continuity of surfaces relative to the human scale. This property deals with the distance from the perceiver, either in terms of direct or indirect reach, and direction relative to our body orientation: front, back, right, left, up and down. Our tactile awareness of walls and doors, compression and expansion provide the 'bodily measurements' (Scott, 1999, p. 228) with which people understand space. Taking a detour from the Bad Oeyn-hausen narrative, two scores of the Tofuku-ji temple ensemble in Kyoto highlight the difference between the visual and haptic properties of space. While the material differences between built area, park area and garden in Bad Oeynhausen puts an emphasis on the visual aspects of the sequence, the Kyoto suburb, the Tofuku-ji temple ensemble and the temple garden are all composed of white stucco walls, gabled roofs, trees, gravel and wood. These architectural components have a similar visual appearance (at least to the Western eye), but the spatial proportions show a contrast between the half-open suburban landscape and the defined enclosures of the temple ensemble that goes beyond the visual image. Contrary to the filmic sequence of discrete moments that the visual score presents, these non-visual spatial dynamics can be represented as a continuous diagram, representing the change in measure of enclosure (Fig. 7).

Returning to Bad Oeynhausen, several kinaesthetic and auditory cues complement and augment the image sequence: the rising and falling of the surface of the earth, the meandering and curving of the path, and the sequence of sounds, with the roaring fountain of the Wasserkrater as the grand finale, reflecting the splashing Jordansprudel at the beginning. The transition from urban area to wooded valley is seen as well as felt by a tight combination of climbing and descending, a sharp change in direction, a quick succession of material changes and an intensification of quality as well as quality of sound.

The locomotion score addresses these dynamic properties of the ground plane, which can be perceived through ascent and descent, moving left or right, straight ahead or turning back, factors of the site which influence bodily position, as interpreted by the vestibular organ. The resulting orientation leads the body to seek a symmetrical balance, and our senses are always directed to that end. Landscape features are often described by names that reflect this 'muscular consciousness', such as a road to be 'climbing' a hill or 'descending' into a valley, as though 'the road itself has muscles, or rather, counter-muscles', as Gaston Bachelard writes (1958/1994, p. 11). For analysing the locomotion score, the vestibular organ is used as measuring device and then removed from the representation, in the same way instruments are not shown when presenting results. The line of movement towards the Wasserkrater garden meanders slightly in the valley, in the park it is constructed of straight path sections and finally in the

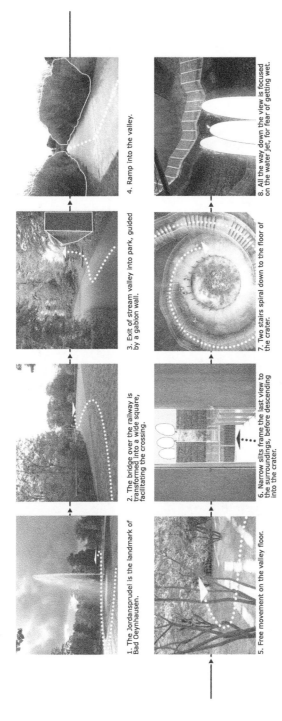

Fig. 6. Visual Score of the Walk From the Jordansprudel to the Wasserkrater. The route is indicated by a dotted line, the objects that frame the space and guide the direction are highlighted by a continuous line, and the elements that catch the eye are shown as a white volume.

1. The Jordansprudel is the landmark of Bad Oeynhausen.

2. The bridge over the railway is transformed into a wide square, facilitating the crossing.

3. Exit of stream valley into park, guided by a gabion wall.

4. Ramp into the valley.

5. Free movement on the valley floor.

6. Narrow slits frame the last view to the surroundings, before descending into the crater.

7. Two stairs spiral down to the floor of the crater.

8. All the way down the view is focused on the water jet, for fear of getting wet.

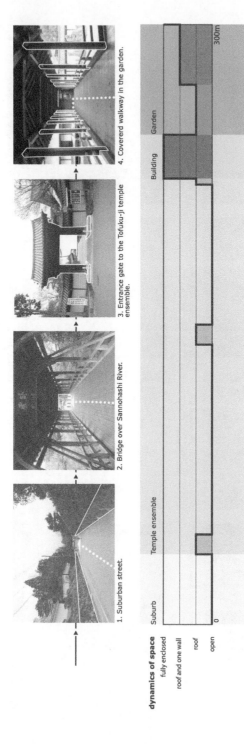

Fig. 7. Visual Score and Haptic Score of the Tofuku-ji Temple Ensemble in Kyoto. The haptic score shows how each transition from one area to another is marked by an enclosure, and how the sizes of the spaces become smaller toward the garden.

garden it is transformed into a spiralling movement, gently at first in the path of stepping stones and then more forceful in the spiral staircases, as an expression of the downward movement. Likewise, in the garden the height differences become larger and steeper and are architecturally elaborated as stairs and ramps (Fig. 8).

The accessory plane that defines the haptic dimensions of space is the surface underfoot. As the primary physical platform for locomotion and spatial perception, the surface underfoot is the most direct embodied contact with the space around us, guiding our position in space. It is the material we feel all the time when moving through space without making a conscious effort, which helps us in finding our way, guiding our direction, recognising where we are. As Ana Luz (2008) concluded in her research on groundscapes, the surface underfoot reflects the environment we are in, and cues in surface material can provide functional information such as hazards or boundaries, differences in programmes of use and domains of private or public thresholds. The material underfoot can also function as a prompt to movement. In many cases, material qualities of different textures, the directionality and scale of the material form and pattern can (un)intentionally send the message to move on or encourage a person to stay and pause for a while. To be interpreted as a prompt, pavement form does not need to be particularly eye-catching or obvious. People perceive the ground they walk on without seeing it, and it is precisely the hidden location of the ground, in its non-frontal way of seeing, that opens up our perception of the world (p. 96). The surface underfoot score documents these properties, including texture, roughness or smoothness and details of surface variation. Firm surfaces require little attention to negotiate; the more muscular and vestibular effort they require, the more awareness of one's surroundings they provide. On one end of the scale are smooth and slippery surfaces, and on the other end, soft, bumpy, loose or rocky surfaces. The transitions from town to valley to park to garden are underscored by material transitions, and the alternation of loose and hard materials underfoot gives the route a rhythmic undertone, which, parallel to the locomotion score, culminates in the moment one enters the garden: steeper slopes, stronger curves and more unstable surface (Fig. 9).

The auditory score represents most explicitly how the Wasserkrater garden, although physically distant, is intimately connected to the town and its origins. The sound of the Wasserkrater recalls the Jordansprudel, with its alternation of sound and quiet, and its drowning of all surrounding sounds. Near the Jordansprudel in town, the sound of the water is so loud that nothing else can be heard, but already at a little distance it merges with the daily urban sounds – a tolling church bell, people and cars. In the valley and the park, the sound of birds forms a continuous background. The Wasserkrater fountain provides the most conspicuous sound on the plain, but its volume does not rise above the volume of the background sounds of the almost continuous airplanes, of the intensive bird singing, of children playing and people talking. Its sounds may be heard at about 50 metres from the edge of the sunken garden, but only inside the garden the fountain is clearly audible. In the intervals between the eruptions of the fountain, the sunken garden appears to be quieter than the surrounding plain, although the sound level is only slightly lower – the volume of the fountain indeed becomes

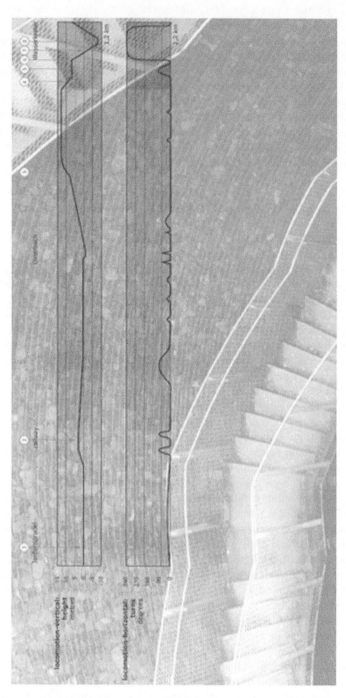

Fig. 8. Locomotion Scores. The sequence from built-up area, valley, park to garden is indicated in shifting shades. The vertical movement is shown in meters, the horizontal changes in direction are shown in degrees. The abrupt changes in height and direction are an intensification of the gradual changes in the urban landscape.

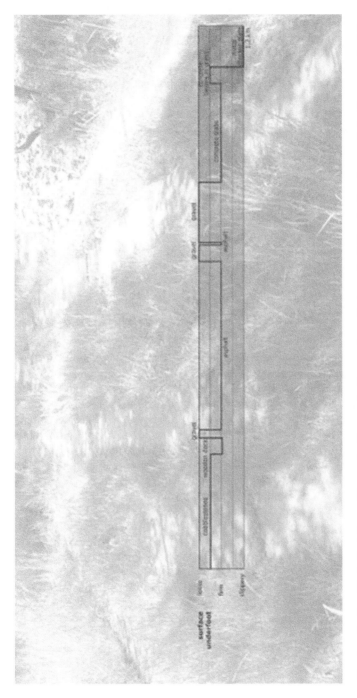

Fig. 9. Surface Underfoot Score. The centre line marks firm surfaces that require little attention to negotiate. On one end of the scale are smooth and slippery surfaces, and on the other soft, bumpy, loose or rocky surfaces that require more muscular and vestibular effort.

louder, but the high-pitched background sounds (the human vocal sounds) become muffled; the bird sounds and the wind remain. Here, the tree canopy muffles the sound of the water, while the hard materials inside the crater echo the thundering sound of the fountain and sharpen the sound of the falling water on the stairs. Only within the confines of the crater wall, where the background sounds have disappeared altogether, the differences between the sound levels of the eruptions and the intervals are substantial, and down at the crater floor the different stages of the soundscape can be clearly distinguished. In the intervals the dripping becomes audible, a sharp rattle on the metal stairs, gradually lessening until the fountain erupts again: a heavy bubbling raises the sound level, rising even more, followed by a sound explosion, retained by the enclosure of the space. The score shows how intimately related auditory information is to spatial composition: only when entering the open space of the park, the wind becomes noticeable, and the little 'hiccup' in the score indicates the narrow entrance to the crater: the acoustic space of the fountain is to a great extent determined by the geometry of the garden, making it aurally perceptible. The impact of the fountain on the soundscape draws the attention from the visual to the multi-sensory qualities of the garden (Fig. 10).

7. CONCLUSION – FROM KINAESTHESIA TO SYNAESTHESIA

The perceivable form of the urban landscape is more than its architecture and more than volumes or voids defined by a series of surfaces. It consists of physical as well as ephemeral and structural components. John Dixon Hunt (2017) wrote: 'We must evade simple reliance on architectural forms. Movement determines mood. The mood is lost when we just look at forms' (p. 13). The perceivable form concerns the shapes, dimensions and proportions of space, and the materiality, the plasticity of topography, planting, and buildings, their visual, haptic and acoustic properties, as well as the interrelations between them which can only perceived in movement. The human body can explore space only by moving through it; it needs perception in order to move, but perception depends on our moving through space at the same time.

Moving through space not only exposes kinaesthetic information that can be derived directly from the movement itself, but all kinds of interwoven, synaesthetic information. Synaesthesia literally means 'joining of the senses'. Neuropsychological theories of synaesthesia treat the phenomenon of intersensoriality (hearing colours or seeing sounds and other such forms of cross-modal stimulation) as a rare genetic condition which has to do with the brains of certain individuals being 'cross-wired'. However, synaesthesia is something that happens on a daily basis and in daily life. The physical environment feels ineluctably tactile, even though we touch only a small part of it. Tactile experience, the sensation in the skin or muscles, also includes the kind of visual experience that leads to anticipate these tactile qualities of the surroundings – seeing the spray of water makes one imagine getting wet and hearing it roar creates a mental image

Fig. 10. Auditory Score. The different sounds of falling water, traffic, birdsong, human voices and wind gain importance in turn.

of a fountain. The muscle effort to bridge a distance provides a sense of space interconnected with perspectival, auditory and tactile information. The sensory faculties are inseparable; they are linked in a multi-directional interaction where one sensation follows another to form different patterns of experience (Howes, 2006; Tuan, 1993, p. 43).

What the combined visual and haptic scores show is how this synaesthetic faculty can be translated from the perceiver to the perceived: the way we can derive meaning from the urban environment. The images, or even the experiences of the urban landscape, only provide meaning by their interrelation, in a sequence of bodily perceived moments (kinaesthesia). Where the perception of the urban environment is often reduced to a visual one, the condensation of haptic cues in the urban landscape makes it a synaesthetically perceived sequence of ambiances, where a combined input of changes in light, textures, sounds and dimensions of space are joined into one. Such representations of movement are valuable in the sense that they expose not the movements themselves, not the subjective experience, perception, or meanings, but the conditions that the urban landscape offers, the qualities that change as we move through them, thus communicating the experiential aspects of urban landscape. In other words, although the faculties of the human body are used as measuring device, the focus, the content, of such analysis is the urban environment. It is an essential quality of these multi-sensory cues that they are not defined images with an associated meaning; they are bodily perceivable kinaesthetic events, which remain abstract in the sense that they do not dictate the relation between urbanites and their environment, but allow for each inhabitant, visitor and researcher to perceive, create and allow to evolve their own narrative.

REFERENCES

Appleyard, D., Lynch, K., & Myer, J. R. (1964). *The view from the road.* Cambridge, MA: MIT Press.
Bachelard, G. (1994). *The poetics of space.* Translated by M. Jolas. Boston, MA: Beacon Press. Originally published as La poétique de l'espace (Presses Universitaires de France, 1958).
Bacon, E. (1974). *Design of cities* (Revised ed.). New York, NY: Viking Press.
Berleant, A. (1997). *Living in the landscape: Towards an aesthetics of environment.* Lawrence, KS: University Press of Kansas.
Bloomer, K. C., & Moore, C. (1977). *Body, memory and architecture.* New Haven, CT: Yale University Press.
Cullen, G. (1961). *The concise townscape.* New York, NY: Reinhold Publishing Corporation.
De Wit, S. I. (2018). *Hidden landscapes: The metropolitan garden as a multi-sensory expression of place.* Amsterdam: Architectura & Natura Press.
Gibson, J. J. (1966). *The senses considered as perceptual systems.* Boston, MA: Houghton Mifflin.
Granö, O., & Paassi, A. (Eds.) (1997). M. Hicks (Trans.). *Pure geography.* Baltimore; London: The Johns Hopkins University Press. Original edition 1929.
Halprin, L. (1969). *The RSVP cycles; creative processes in the human environment.* New York, NY: George Braziller.
Havik, K., Notteboom, B., & de Wit, S. I. (2017). Narrating urban landscapes [Editorial]. *OASE, 98,* 1–8.
Hayden, D. (1995). *The power of place: Urban landscapes as public history.* Cambridge, MA: The MIT Press.

Howes, D. (2006). Scent, sound and synaesthesia; intersensoriality and material culture theory. In C. Tilley, W. Keane, S. Kuechler, M. Rowlands & P. Spyer (Eds.), *Handbook of material culture.* London; Washington, DC: Sage.

Hunt, J. D. (2003). "Lordship of the feet": Towards a poetics of movement in the garden. In M. Conan (Ed.), *Landscape design and the experience of motion, Dumbarton Oaks Colloquium on the history of landscape architecture* (pp. 187–214). Washington, DC: Dumbarton Oaks, Trustees for Harvard University.

Hunt, J. D. (2017). Beyond Ekphrasis, beyond sight, beyond words. . .. In D. F. Ruggles (Ed.), *Sound and scent in the garden. Dumbarton Oaks Colloquium on the history of landscape architecture* (Vol. 38, pp. 13–30). Washington, DC: Dumbarton Oaks Research Library and Collection.

Lassus, B. (1998). *The landscape approach.* Philadelphia, PA: University of Pennsylvania Press.

Luz, A. (2008). On pavements and other public groundscapes. Ground as Canvas for and process of urban exploration in design processes. *OASE # 77 Into the open,* 91–100.

Malnar, J. M., & Vodvarka, F. (2004). *Sensory design.* Minneapolis, MN: University of Minnesota Press.

Massey, D. (1993). Power-geometry and a progressive sense of place. In J. Bird, B. Curtis, T. Putnam, & L. Tickner (Eds.), *Mapping the future: Local cultures, global change* (pp. 27–37). New York, NY: Routledge.

Paterson, M. (2009). Haptic geographies: Ethnography, haptic knowledges and sensuous dispositions. *Progress in Human Geography, 33*(6), 766–788.

Peterson, S. K. (1980). Space and anti-space. *Harvard Architecture Review, Spring,* 88–113.

Quantrill, M. (1987). *The environmental memory.* New York, NY: Schocken Books.

Scott, G. (1999). *The architecture of humanism: A study in the history of taste.* New York, NY: W. W. Norton Company.

Smithson, R. (1967). The monuments of Passaic. *Artforum, VI*(4), 48–51.

Solnit, R. (2001). *Wanderlust: A history of walking.* London: Granta Books.

Tuan, Y.-F. (1993). *Passing strange and wonderful.* Washington, DC: Island Press.

Walter, E. V. (1988). *Placeways: A theory of the human environment.* Chapel Hill, NC: University of North Carolina Press.

Chapter 3

THE VISUAL COMMONS: WHERE RESIDENTS BECOME NEIGHBORS

Jon Wagner

ABSTRACT

The concept of a "visual commons" ties together two key dimensions of how people live together: the expression and pursuit of individual and collective interests, and the expression and development of how residents see and visualize where they live. This concept has helped me think more critically about the relative contributions of cognitive maps, collective perspectives, and symbolic interaction to community studies. It's also been useful in revealing the visual ground against which residents figure the process of becoming neighbors and the disconnects that follow in how residents see where they're living and the natural environments they live within.

Keywords: Community; ecology; neighborhood; urban wildlife; visualization; worldmaking

How do people see where they live? What visual images of their neighborhood do they develop and share with other residents? How and when might they do that? And how might shared visualizations – both real and imagined – encourage residents to regard each other as neighbors?

These questions emerged for me within a long-term visual study I have been conducting of Thousand Oaks, a residential area on the East Side of San Francisco Bay where I've now lived for over 40 years. As this study evolved, I became more and more attuned to the vitality residents found in actively "seeing" and commenting about how things looked in and around where they lived. Beyond the vitality itself, talking about "how things looked" seemed to draw residents into a shared perspective that I will refer to in this essay as the "visual commons" (Fig. 1).

Visual and Multimodal Urban Sociology, Part B
Research in Urban Sociology, Volume 18B, 63–101
Copyright © 2023 by Emerald Publishing Limited
All rights of reproduction in any form reserved
ISSN: 1047-0042/doi:10.1108/S1047-00422023000018B003

Fig. 1. Thousand Oaks.
This street level view is from near the center of the neighborhood looking eastward,
away from the Bay and up towards the hills. *Source:* Photo by Jon Wagner.

The "visual commons" can be viewed as the overlap among residents' individual visualizations of where they live and as a symbolic space in which those
visualizations are shared. In both respects, it foregrounds the importance to
individuals and groups of how they see where they live. As a form of local
worldmaking, the visual commons can also help or hinder residents in trying to
align images of their neighborhood with the de facto natural communities they
live within.

1. COMMUNITIES AND VISUAL STUDIES

When I moved to Thousand Oaks in 1976, it was a relatively sleepy, aging, and
largely white middle-class residential area. Many residents were retired and had lived
here for years, some since the 1920s and 1930s. The one commercial artery through
the area, Solano Avenue, boasted a fair-sized hardware and house goods store, two
movie theaters, two highly regarded ice cream stores, several Chinese restaurants, a
grocery supermarket, a "Telephone Market" – that nearby residents could call to
deliver produce and canned goods – and various gift shops, real estate agencies,
banks, beauty and barber shops, cleaners, and so on (see Fig. 2).

Fig. 2. Solano Avenue.
The area's primary commercial artery cuts through neighborhoods that are otherwise
entirely residential. *Source:* Photo by Google Earth.

During the 45 years I've lived here, the number of restaurants has increased
more than tenfold. A few chain stores arrived, and some independent shops
disappeared, including the two ice cream and coffee shops, both of which had
loyal patrons (but so do the Peet's and Starbucks that replaced them). One movie
house also closed for renovation as a rock climbing and exercise center. As the
area became increasingly upscale, "The Avenue" developed a regional reputation
for its many restaurants and boutiques. There are only three traffic lights from
top to bottom, but automobile traffic is now slowed by diverters, "bump out"
parklets, and complex lane markers. Beginning in 1976, the mile-long Avenue has
been closed to traffic for one day each September for a street festival that, in
recent years, has attracted 100,000 or more people (see Fig. 3).

Throughout the same 45 years, neighborhoods on both sides of Solano
Avenue have remained exclusively residential. Though a few small apartment
buildings adjoin the Avenue, most residents live in detached, single-family homes.
Many were built almost 100 years ago, and most have been renovated multiple
times since. The pace of remodeling accelerated in the last 20 years, and in 2021
home prices and rents were at an all-time high. Most residents are white, but the
population has become more diverse as families with Latinx, Middle Eastern,
East Asian, Asian, and mixed roots have moved into the area.

Before moving to Thousand Oaks, I'd worked for several years with Suzanne
Keller to design and implement the photographic component of her multiyear
field study of Twin Rivers, New Jersey (Keller, 2003). In that study we photo-
documented key settings, scenes, signs, embellishments, and destructions of the
built environment, and we used photographs as prompts for interviewing

Fig. 3. The "Solano Stroll."
Solano Avenue is packed with people for an annual street festival that local businesses began hosting in 1976. *Source:* Photo by Jon Wagner.

residents about how they saw where they lived (Wagner, 1979a). I left that project with an appreciation of image-based fieldwork, a sense that communities were significant forms of social organization, and an interest in conducting a visual study of another one. Shortly after settling in Thousand Oaks, I began photographing my new neighborhood and the surrounding area with just that in mind (Fig. 4).

To guide our photographic work in Twin Rivers, Keller and I derived what Suchar (1997) has called a "shooting script" from her working theory about community life. And in Thousand Oaks, I initially included several elements from that script – e.g., signage and visible changes residents made to their homes and yards. But I also photographed whatever I found visually interesting that might help me understand how residents saw where they lived.

This inductive approach led me to notice and document visual details in Thousand Oaks that we never thought to examine in Twin Rivers (Wagner, 2016). Beginning in 2010, I also worked toward comparing what was photographically visible in Thousand Oaks (as an outside or "etic" perspective) with visual images and visualizations that residents themselves acquired, developed, and shared about the neighborhood (an "emic" perspective). Exploring these complementary perspectives in Thousand Oaks eventually led me to the "visual commons" as a neighborhood alternative to the concept of community I'd started with.

Fig. 4. Scripted Photo-Documents.
I took the top photos according to a script for documenting how Twin Rivers residents used physical spaces for purposes unintended by the town's planners: a parking lot as a meeting place (top left) and a common lawn area as a community garden (top right). I took the bottom two photos to explore the visibility (or invisibility) of property lot lines (photo on left) and how residents managed and arranged discarded materials (on the right). Themes for the bottom photos emerged inductively as I photographed whatever might help me understand how residents saw where they lived. *Source:* Photos by Jon Wagner.

2. A VISUAL LANDSCAPE BEHELD PARTLY IN COMMON

As part of the Twin Rivers study, I designed and conducted a randomized sampling of the town's visible features (Keller, 1976; Wagner, 1979b). While experimenting with similar strategies in Thousand Oaks, I identified five physical features that visibly dominated street-level views: streets and sidewalks, "easement" spaces between the streets and sidewalks, automobiles, houses, and vegetation (trees, bushes, lawns, and gardens). From almost any spot in the neighborhood, a pedestrian's field of view at eye level in any direction would likely include two or more of these five features, any one which could account for a larger portion of the view than anything else.

Each of these visually dominant features has a different provenance, but legal ownership for three is relatively unambiguous. Sidewalks and streets are owned by the city, and both homes and automobiles are owned (or leased) by individual residents (with a few ride-share exceptions). Ownership of easement spaces and of trees and large shrubs, however, is frequently unclear. Easement land is owned by the city, and residents are restricted in what they can do with it. But residents are responsible for maintaining the easement space that fronts their own lots. These ambiguities frame easements as contested strips of liminal space between every street and sidewalk in Thousand Oaks (see Fig. 5).

Trees and large shrubs are another visibly dominant feature of the Thousand Oaks neighborhood. They are noticeable when looking up, down or across almost any street or sidewalk in the area. They are also frequently visible overhead (see Figs. 5 and 6). The size, coloring texture, and form of trees and shrubs stand out from the uniform surface of streets and sidewalks. From many vantage points their branches and foliage also block views of houses and cars.

In contrast to homes, automobiles, and city streets, the ownership of trees and shrubs is frequently open to question, making them easier to associate with the neighborhood as a whole. Roots and branches can grow into or across adjoining yards, walkways, and streets, and, from a distance, it's difficult to see where larger trees are rooted. Ambiguities are compounded for trees growing on the easement strips, where most trees lining Thousand Oaks streets were initially planted. Trees and bushes that grow higher than houses add even more ambiguity

Fig. 5. A Neighbor's Warning.
A resident's signs alert passersby to the danger and politics of falling palm fronds from trees rooted in the easement between sidewalk and street. *Source:* Photos by Lynne Hollingsworth.

Fig. 6. Defining Vertical Space.
The branches of this forty-foot tall tree animate and shape the vertical space above its trunk and the surrounding residences. *Source:* Photo by Jon Wagner.

by calling attention to the three-dimensional space above streets, houses, and yards that in no clear way is attached to any of them.

By hosting other forms of wild life – birds, racoons, squirrels, and so on – trees also appear as icons and embodiments of the natural world. Looking up into such a tree reveals a materialized three-dimensional form that, if constructed by a human being, would be totally at odds with local building codes. And relative to the human community in which those codes are generated, trees are decidedly unruly. As living members of an ecological community, however, their physical structure is an orderly expression of genetic inheritance and natural setting. Neighborhood residents and city administrators may serve as custodians of that setting, but it's not something they own. Other forms of vegetation in Thousand Oaks suggest much the same, including shrubs, grasses, and vines that grow beyond where they have been planted and into sidewalks and roadways.

For all these reasons, trees can and do appear to local residents not only as greenery but also as a neighborhood or community resource that is, at times, worth fighting for – or at least worrying about. As this became clearer to me, I wondered if collective awareness of Thousand Oaks trees might engender among residents a sense of community. If so, I also wondered if within that sensibility trees were solely visual attractions, or viewed also in ecological terms – as stable, slow-moving, and productive residents of the locality in which they grew. I didn't hear much about that from Thousand Oaks residents, and I came to wonder about that as well.

Trees are not the only visible features in Thousand Oaks that might express or engender communitarian sensibilities among neighborhood residents. The same can be said about the signs residents post on or near their homes to communicate with neighbors and others passing by. Evidence that people are living "together" in the Thousand Oaks area also appears in efforts by residents to prepare for natural disasters, annual block parties, and other social gatherings, including memorial services for neighbors who passed away. Indeed, as home to varied forms of life, Thousand Oaks is a physical setting in which people can observe together the growth, pace and passing of seasons, plants, animals, and of neighborhood residents themselves. And, in sharing stories of what they see of such changes, residents implicitly affirm their shared interest in "how things look" (see Fig. 7).

3. COMMUNITY STUDIES AND THE VISUAL COMMONS

The vitality of resident stories about what they were seeing in Thousand Oaks led me to the idea that the visualizations people develop of where they live shape their thoughts, feelings, behavior, and real or imagined connections with other people who live nearby – and do so somewhat independently. That idea was the ground against which I recognized the "visual commons" as a neglected dimension of otherwise traditional community studies (Wagner, 2014).

To further refine this idea, I revisited my personal collection of community studies, including Keller's culminating (2003) examination of Twin Rivers and Gerald Suttles' (1968, 1972) multiyear explorations of two Chicago neighborhoods. Both Keller and Suttles were thoughtful and literate sociologists who regarded territory and landscape as potentially defining features of community life, but they located their studies within somewhat different historical arcs. Keller drew inspiration from the Greek "polis" and classic sociologists such as Ferdinand Tonnies and Emile Durkheim and their implications for developing new communities. Suttles oriented his work toward evolving concepts of community in the modern era and the challenge of sustaining social order among diverse populations. Both linked their ideas to empirical evidence, but in somewhat different ways.

In Community (2003) Keller affirms the value of enduring, socially engaging, and place-based communities to a healthy society and individual well-being. She displays in Fig. 8 what a well-realized example of this ideal would include and

Fig. 7. Resident Signs.
These signs posted by residents for neighbors and passersby call attention to, from top to bottom, left to right: George Floyd's death; a deliberately "wild," (not neglected) yard; parallels between racism and the covid-19 virus; a memorial sunflower planting for a recently deceased resident; and the responsibility of strangers (two signs) to respect resident landscaping. *Source:* Photos by Jon Wagner.

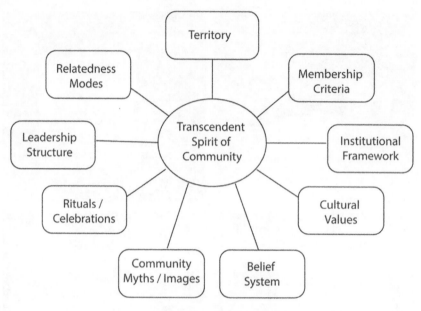

Fig. 8.   "Building Blocks of Community".
Source: Adapted from Keller (2003, p. 265). By permission of Princeton University Press.

argues as much by wedding a comment from Doheny-Farina (1996) with a few thoughts of her own:

> 'A community is bound by place [and] complex social and environmental necessities. It is not something you can easily join.' One cannot subscribe to it. 'It must be lived. It is entwined, contradictory, and it and involves all the senses – and long acquaintance.' Communities need a center and a heart as well as a public arena where public discourse and actions can take place. To be 'rooted in a community, one must spend a long time integrating one's life into a place.' (Keller, Op.cit. p. 298)

Keller's scholarship is thoughtful and well informed, but the "building blocks" displayed in Fig. 8 appear to be equally important and universally essential. Are they? For everyone? The block labels are intriguing, but why not call them dimensions that could be more or less prominent in different kinds of communities? It seems likely to me that, in reality, they would be, and that different kinds of communities might serve some people better than others. If so, why emphasize the enduring value of the full set?

Part of the answer is Keller's choice to examine the concept of community as an "ideal type" rather than a composition of ethnographic studies or a multivocal narrative (e.g., Alexievich, 2006/1997; Myerhoff, 1978; or Terkel, 2006). Since Max Weber's seminal use of the term, ideal types have been popular and well-regarded tools for linking social theory with empirical evidence. But for Keller, the idea of a full-featured community is "ideal" in moral, as well as analytical, terms. That's implicit in her comparison of communitarian ideals with individualistic pathologies such as anomie, alienation, isolation, and loneliness. An even-handed approach would compare both ideals and pathologies of each. It also appears in her emphasis on community engagement as cause and remedy for those pathologies, to the relative neglect of poverty, job loss, workplace des-killing, racial and gender discrimination, child-rearing practices, and so on.

Keller not only champions communities, she also trivializes individual rela-tionships. "Coffee breaks, friendly exchanges around water coolers, conviviality in urban pocket parks all serve a purpose, but they are not of lasting conse-quence" (2003, p. 298). Perhaps, but what moments alone cannot sustain the relationships they engender sometimes can. That's something we might miss if we start with an idealized version of community in mind. It's also worth asking how her ideal typical "community" compares with other forms of place-based asso-ciation, some of which make a hash of Fig. 8.

In the interest of full disclosure, for over 40 years now I have lived in the same house and neighborhood, and I can see what attracted Keller to the ideal of an enduring and full-featured community. However, by the time I was 30 years old, I also had lived for three months or more in 20 different towns and 34 different houses or apartments. Given all that moving around, Keller's ideal of a stable and comprehensive community seems more quaint than robust.

Closer to my experience (and my field studies) is Gerald Suttles' notion of a community as a two-level locus of opportunities for human connection:

'First, there is the physical structure of the city; the location of its facilities, residential groups, transportation and communication lines; and its specialized activities. . . Second, there is the cognitive map, which residents have for describing, not only what their city is like, but what they think it ought to be like' (1968, p. 22)

And, as Suttles notes, these cognitive maps "need not necessarily correspond closely with the actual physical structure" (Fig. 9).

Both Keller and Suttles bounded their studies with physical features of a "known" community and the territory associated with it. But where would their studies have taken them if they started instead by asking questions about how residents see where they live? I'm not sure, but probably not with maps like these – and perhaps not even with the concept of a "community."

Something like the concept I'm referring to as a "visual commons" could be derived from the building blocks Keller labeled "myth and image" and "turf/ territory." It's less of a stretch, however, to build out from Suttles' notion of a resident's "cognitive map" toward more complex visualizations based on remembered and imagined images, episodes, commentaries, and views. Indeed, I inferred the existence of a "visual commons" from the desire and vitality Thousand Oaks residents brought to expressing and comparing visualizations of this sort. As the symbolic space where residents could imagine that kind of sharing, and the context of neighborhood storytelling, the attractions of such a "commons" were similar to those Suttles (1972) attributes to local communities themselves:

...like all other institutions, the local community attracts to itself additional hopes for the expression of self and sentiment. The desire to find a social setting in which one can give rein to an authentic version of oneself and see other people as they really are is not some unanalyzable human need but the most fundamental way in which people are reassured of their own reality as

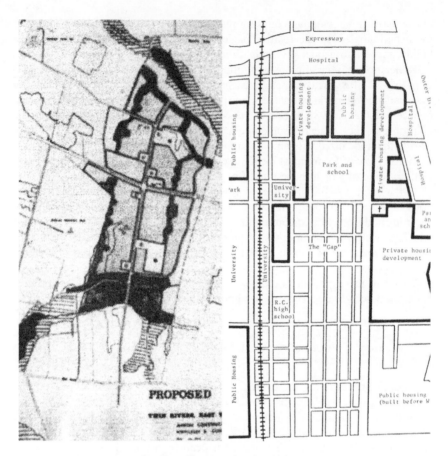

Fig. 9.   Community Area Maps.
On the left is a map of what would become Twin Rivers (from Keller, 2003, p. 53, by
permission from Princeton University Press). On the right is a map of the Douglas
area of Chicago that Gerald Suttles studied (from Suttles, 1972, p. 85, by permission
of University of Chicago Press). These stylized maps foreground boundary and path
information useful for travelers, business interests, institutional service providers, and
property owners, but they're a far cry from the kind of multi-dimensional and richly
layered "cognitive maps" residents develop and draw upon to understand, navigate
and find meaning where they live.

> well as that of other people. . . Presentations of self, then, are not mere ways of letting off steam:
> they are essential expressive interludes when group members reestablish each others' confidence
> in the coincidence between subjective and objective realities. (Suttles, 1972, pp. 264–265)

My explorations in Thousand Oaks suggest that both real and imagined
"expressive interludes" among residents about how they see where they live are as
fundamental and essential as those described by Suttles – and for many of the
same reasons.

4. LEGAL BOUNDARIES AND VISIBLE FEATURES

My interest in how residents of Thousand Oaks visualized where they live was heightened after reviewing the Country Recorder's parcel maps for the area (see Fig. 10 for a small section of one). The parcel maps demarcate clear-cut boundaries between properties owned by the municipal government and by private individuals (who typically acquire a parcel of land when purchasing the home on which it is sited). The maps revealed that every square inch (literally!) of the area in which I live is legally owned by the city and individual home owners. Residents and landlords own the lots, and the city owns the streets, sidewalks, and "easement" spaces between sidewalks and the street. The people living in this neighborhood may or may not experience a sense of community or collective identity, but their legal standing is that of individual property owners (not as a group) who invested in a small chunk of land.

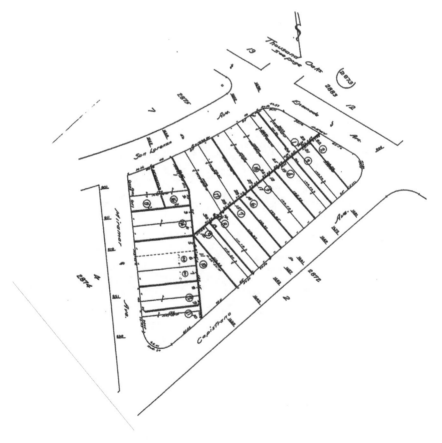

Fig. 10.   Parcel Map Section: Alameda County.
This section of the Alameda County parcel map covers a typical housing block in the Thousand Oaks neighborhood. (Public Domain).

Other than the territory itself, I also found nothing about the parcel maps to suggest that the neighborhood was a "community" characterized by Keller's "building blocks" (see Fig. 8). There were no community properties, no references to community access or events or history, and no indications of which schools or churches or businesses might be serving the area.

The parcel maps do refer to the Thousand Oaks area, and we could attribute to people who lived there a collective identity, but that might or might not reflect their experience. Borrowing a distinction from Marx, it's not evident from the parcel maps that people who live in Thousand Oaks are a neighborhood "in" itself, let alone "for" itself.

Google Earth photos (see Fig. 11) of the same area, however, reveal clusters of dense vegetation that make it difficult if not impossible to see the same property boundaries from the air – in many cases at street level as well. This vegetation is a visible symbol that life can and does unfold in Thousand Oaks outside the institutional boundaries defined by property rights and municipal regulation.

Other evidence of that possibility appears when residents themselves cross property boundaries to socialize; attend neighborhood meetings; house-sit for each other; care for children, the elderly, pets, and plants; or respond to local emergencies. Compared to the constant visual reminders of the neighborhood's

Fig. 11.   Parcel Map Section: Aerial View.
This photograph depicts the same physical area as the parcel map section in
Fig. 10. *Source*: Photo by Google Earth.

vegetation, however, this cross-lot social behavior is transitory and visible primarily to participants. On the basis of this comparison, we could say that visible social life in Thousand Oaks comes and goes, but the earth and the neighborhood trees rooted therein more or less abide.

In the aerial photograph (Fig. 11), the mass of vegetation at the center is the largest distinguishable figure, but there's no evidence of that on the parcel maps. And, while the trees making up that mass can be shaped and pruned by residents, they cross over between one lot and another according to their own growth patterns, without regard for property rights or municipal regulations. By living "outside" property lines, trees in Thousand Oaks can appear as a visual resource held in common by anyone who can see them.

5. RESIDENT TREES AND OTHER FLORA

The aerial view in Fig. 11 may be unfamiliar to many residents, but the taller trees within the center cluster tower over houses and are also visible at street level from vantage points all around the block (Fig. 12). Seen from above or from the street, this tree mass makes visible a three-dimensional space that no one can appropriate and everyone can see.

Fig. 12.   Parcel Map Section: Street View.
This photograph offers a street level view of the same block represented in the parcel map (Fig. 10) and the aerial view (Fig. 11). *Source:* Photo by Jon Wagner.

Shrubs and other dense vegetation can play a similar role on a smaller scale. Their growth and presence is less dramatic than large trees in calling attention to the neighborhood's vertical "free" space, but they do quite well at blurring property lines between adjacent residences. Overgrown lot lines create an opportunity for residents to imaginatively extend their personal living space to include everything they can see. Considered together, I came to regard resident visualizations of this extended space as a kind of "visual commons" that residents care about as individuals, but create collectively – an imaginary landscape that is real in its social and ecological consequences.

Thousand Oaks trees also can help residents know where they are – and when (see Figs. 13, 14, 15, 16). The palm trees in Figs. 13 and 14 are visible for several blocks in every direction and make the neighborhood more "imageable" (Lynch, 1960) than it would be otherwise. The distinctive tree-obscured home on the right in Fig. 14 can also serve as a location marker for anyone who recognizes it, and

Fig. 13.   Unruly Trees.
The trees visible in this photo are growing in, above, and across more than a dozen different parcels of privately owned land, but the only visible evidence of property boundaries from this vantage point are a few sections of fence. *Source:* Photo by Jon Wagner.

Fig. 14. Imageable and Legible Trees. *Source:* Photos by Jon Wagner.

Fig. 15. How Trees Shape Views.
The tree on the left dominates the view from this vantage point. It visually absorbs the utility lines running overhead, hides the homes and hills behind it from view, and frames the negative space in front of it. The tree on the right forms an arbor that separates pedestrians from the street (on the right) and houses (to the left). During sunny days, this tree also casts dramatic shadows across a section of sidewalk that, without the tree, would appear as open and exposed as the sidewalk on the left.
Source: Photos by Jon Wagner.

Fig. 16.   Visual Dominance.
These trees dominate the view from across this street and hide completely the two
houses behind them. Like many other trees in Thousand Oaks, they're rooted in an
easement strip. If you asked a resident who owns them, the most likely response would
be "no one." *Source:* Photo by author; Photo by Jon Wagner.

the color of the trees themselves is a "legible" (Lynch, 1960) time stamp by the
seasons.

6. RESIDENT WILDLIFE AND OTHER FAUNA

The visible dominance of trees and shrubs in Thousand Oaks gives the area a
distinctive visual texture and implicitly affirms the notion that residents live
together, rather than separately. This vegetation also provides varied habitats for
different forms of wildlife – deer, possums, raccoons, and coyotes among the
shrubs in larger yards, undeveloped lots and ravines; birds in bushes and small
trees; butterflies and bees among the flowers; and rats in the ivy (see Fig. 17). For
residents, this intersection of flora and fauna animates a shared three-dimensional
space of indeterminate ownership. Within that space, wildlife, insects, the
weather, and the vagaries of earth, air, water, and fire are visibly manifest enough
at times to attract the attention of residents, who then add meaning to where they
live by telling stories about what they see.

In addition to telling stories about neighborhood flora and fauna, residents
also ask questions and tell stories about the appearance of other residents. Some
stories feature changes directly observed, as when someone begins or discontinues
riding a bicycle, walking a dog, or appears in public with strangers wearing

Fig. 17. Thousand Oaks Synanthropes.
Thousand Oaks supports numerous species of wildlife that have adapted to thrive in human communities. These include, (from top left to bottom right): a squirrel running off with a neighbor's baguette, crows, a Covid-19 virus alert on outdoor library boxes, a skunk feeding from a bowl set out by a neighborhood resident, a raccoon killed while crossing a street, and wild turkeys perched on a rooftop. *Source:* Turkey photo by Joan Hollingsworth; All photos by Jon Wagner.

uniforms. Others reflect inferences from visible details: people wearing or not wearing antiviral masks, curtains closed that were formerly always open, or the red blinking lights of an emergency response vehicle heading down the block.

Neighbors can exchange comments about these visible details in a neighborhood email forum, block party, or meeting, but most conversations take place in chance encounters while running errands, doing yard work, taking out the trash or responding to perturbations of the landscape itself: the rush of water from a broken main, removal of a large tree, demolition or construction of a home or city sewer, or a house on fire.

The values implicit in attending to the well-being of other residents align well with traditional notions of community as an engaging, supportive form of social organization. Those values can extend beyond the social realm, however, when residents refer to their own physical and health challenges in terms of "the human condition," or a "stream of life" that, at least implicitly, could include neighborhood animals and plants. In some cases, residents may respond to the illness, injury, or death of a cherished neighborhood plant or animal much as they might to suffering or loss of a resident human being. It is more common, however, for them to see neighborhood plants and animals as signs of life within a neighborhood of people than to see each other as human beings living among the plants and animals (Fig. 18).

The people-centric view that Thousand Oaks residents have of where they live mirrors the emphasis of social research about communities in nonagrarian

Fig. 18.   Dogs and Cats.
Dogs are not allowed to run free in Thousand Oaks. They must be leashed or fenced in, managed or trained to observe some rules of human society, and their human owners (or guardians) are held responsible for their behavior. These institutional regulations do not apply to cats – some of whom enjoy the hospitality of multiple neighbors and are regarded more as community members, or domesticated wildlife, than as pets. *Source:* Photos by Jon Wagner.

societies. This perspective regards neighborhood wildlife as an exotic complement to the domestic core of a human community, but it is "exotic" only to the human, and not to the ecological, community. That presumption may be changing. Increased attention to ecological challenges has made its way into city-zoning and building codes, and residents are held more responsible than they used to be for the natural areas in which they live. Sustaining (or managing) local wildlife could be part of those responsibilities but rarely is.

Many Thousand Oaks residents appreciate the diversity and vitality of the area's trees and wildlife, and some go to great lengths to care for undomesticated plants and animals. Environmental policy efforts, however, are at best loosely coupled to how residents want where they live to look. Curbside recycling is highly valued, even though it brings trash cans into view on streets and sidewalks once a week (a high-visibility location that residents might otherwise find offensive). On the other hand, to enhance "how things look," residents continue to invest in ecologically costly features and practices, including water-intensive landscaping, privately owned cars, open air fires and barbeques, paved walkways and patios, and so on.

7. RESIDENT VIEWS OF WHAT'S NEAR AND DEAR

Erving Goffman argued in Asylums (1961, p. 180) that built into the social arrangements of any organization is a conception of its members, not just as members, but as human beings. He also suggested we consider a person's course through life as the two-sided unfoldings of a "moral career," where "One side is linked to internal matters held dearly and closely, such as image of self and felt identity," and "the other side concerns official position, jural relations, and style of life. . . ." (Goffman, 1961, p. 127)

These propositions about organizations, members, and persons also make good sense in thinking about neighborhoods and their residents. The corresponding institutional and jural relationships that define neighborhoods include municipal boundaries, city regulations, and parcel maps. But where can we look to learn more about the internal matters Goffman refers to, including a sense of what's near and dear to residents themselves?

In Thousand Oaks, I learned a lot about the latter from neighborhood story-telling, dramas, and disagreements that focused on how residents viewed the area in which they lived. A defining example emerged one evening when I heard a loud crash and went outside to find that a half-rotten tree growing in our neighbor Delia's yard had fallen across our fence and apple tree. My first thought was proprietary: Was our fence or apple tree seriously damaged? After determining both were okay, I considered what Delia and I might work out for removing the fallen tree.

What I did not consider initially at all was the effect this fallen tree might have on how the neighborhood looked. For several other neighbors, however, that was a significant concern. Though relatively small, and dwarfed by several other trees, including one five times its size, the fallen tree, while standing, had blocked their view of Delia's trash can. The can was extremely well maintained and over 75 feet away, but it was now visible from their homes if they looked in that direction. Over the next 10 days or so, as the concerns of nearby neighbors were aired through group email messaging, I realized that their interests were just as proprietary as mine. From their perspective (both literal and figurative), my fence and apple tree had survived, but their view had not, and needed to be repaired.

To restore their view into Delia's yard, some neighbors proposed that she plant a new tree. It could be smaller than the one that fell, they argued, but if placed just so, it would block their view of her trash can. Beyond that, some neighbors recommended tree varieties for Delia to consider and volunteered to pay for a new tree and have their own gardener plant it. If Delia wanted to consult a landscape expert, they could arrange that too.

My wife and I were taken aback by how forceful the neighbors were in lobbying Delia. "How can they think they have any right," my wife asked, "to tell Delia what she needs to do when it's not even their yard?"

In the pause before I tried to answer her question, my memory flashed through myriad instances of this kind of across-the-lot-line commentary that we'd previously entered into about fence designs, second story additions, garage demolitions, abandoned cars and houses, cars blocking the sidewalk, misguided tree plantings and removals, the half-repaired bungalow down the block, the hoarder's house filled with rolled-up newspapers, the cactus blocking half the sidewalk, and so on. With all that in mind, I realized that the same question could be asked just as well of the two of us or any of our other neighbors. "Well," I said "I guess people just really want where they live to look the way they want it to look" (Fig. 19).

This was not the answer my wife was looking for, but it crystalized for me an idea – also featured in Dr. Seuss's *Yertle the Turtle* (1958) – that people can develop a sense of ownership for whatever they can see within and around where they live. This sense of ownership is individualized (i.e., what is visible varies from one household to the next) but also collective (i.e., some dimensions of the neighborhood are visible to everyone who lives in or passes through the area). Of particular interest to me, a shared sense of ownership for what is visible around where they live seemed to capture something about the neighborhood that residents held "near and dear." Like memories of a friendship or family gathering, this sense of ownership existed both within the imaginations of individual residents and in relationships with other parties. Like at least some of the neighborhood's flora and fauna, it also showed no respect for property lot lines.

My explorations of Thousand Oaks and other community studies suggested that it was not only possible but also likely that residents develop a proprietary interest in how things look in and around where they live. Where they live and what they notice is certainly shaped by social and economic factors, but "how things look" seemed to independently vitalize how Thousand Oaks residents engaged with each other. I didn't know what to call that engagement, but the term "visual commons" came to mind.

Fig. 19. Meaningful Trees.
Residents' comments about these and other trees revealed some of what they held "near and dear" about where they live. From top to bottom: the tree that fell across our fence; three views of a tree removal – lamented by most residents, but welcomed by neighbors who feared the tree might fall into their yards; severely pruned trees that some residents found amusing, and others unconscionable. As one resident put it, "That's just sick! Who would do something like that to a tree?" *Source:* All photos by Jon Wagner.

8. RESIDENT VISUALIZATIONS

To the extent that large trees, other notable flora and fauna, or individual residents themselves become familiar sights in Thousand Oaks, they can also become conspicuous to residents by their absence. In much the same way, the visual imagery that residents develop of where they live can include elements that are no longer visible – except, as our daughter once noted about a cat who had died, "in photographs and our imaginations."

Along the same lines, the flow of imagery into the kind of "visual commons" I'm proposing is based only in part on objectively visible features of the neighborhood or environment in which residents live. From among all that is visible, residents only see what they notice, or have noticed in the past. Beyond that, residents also "see" where they live currently in conjunction with how they saw, or imagine, living at other times and in other places, either directly or as depicted in stories and images they became acquainted with.

And the improvising and imaginative constructions don't end there. Indeed, the visual images residents develop of where they live can include the whole creative array of fabrications, distortions, and extensions that Nelson Goodman (1978) has described as elements of "worldmaking."

An intriguing example of this kind of worldmaking came my way when our daughter, who had moved to Cleveland for graduate school, asked me for a photograph of the view she'd grown up with from our back deck. When I asked her to clarify what she had in mind, she described in great detail a view that included two palm trees on the right and the Golden Gate Bridge far off in the distance to the left.

The challenge in trying to honor this request was that the view she remembers does not exist. The Golden Gate Bridge cannot be seen from anywhere in, behind, in front of, or on top of our house, and the two palm trees are visible only by looking away from the direction in which the bridge is located. But that's not how our daughter remembers the view she grew up with. What she does remember is something like the image in Fig. 20, which I created by combining parts of three different photographs. The result is a "fake" photograph, but a relatively accurate document of a view my daughter remembers from the neighborhood in which she grew up.

My daughter's request reminded me that what residents see, what they remember, and how they visualize a neighborhood are only loosely coupled – though perhaps in a way that mirrors Goffman's two-sided notion of a moral career: On the one side for residents (analogous to external, jural relationships) are material and visible realities of their neighborhood – the physically objective material world. On the other (analogous to the internal near and dear) are the images and remembrances they acquire and curate in visualizing where they live and how they want it to look.

As another example of these ambiguities, Fig. 21 includes two images that invert the truth value of the composited ("fake") photo in Fig. 20. Residents would likely regard both images in Fig. 21 as accurate, but unrepresentative. On the left, pedestrians and cars are conspicuously absent one evening in March 2020 when businesses on Solano Avenue were shuttered in response to the COVID-19

Fig. 20.   A Remembered but Impossible View. *Source:* Photos and montage
by Jon Wagner.

pandemic. On the right, the midday sun is muted by thick smoke during California's disastrous 2018 fire season.

9. THE NATURE OF URBAN NEIGHBORHOODS

My initial notions of the kind of "community" I was exploring in Thousand Oaks focused on collective social life and communitarian ideals among the people who live here. That's close to the image most of us probably have of a community of neighboring residents. Typically, it's also what we refer to in noting that one community is more or less safe, middle class, diverse, well established, transient, impoverished, or attractive than another.

This focus on human residents, however, is somewhat presumptuous. Human settlements are inevitably embedded within the flora, fauna, geography, geology, and weather of locally distinct ecological communities and linked to their regional, continental, and global counterparts. Initially, I didn't pay much attention in Thousand Oaks to the "natural" community in which residents were de facto living, and they didn't seem to either.

Indeed, my fellow residents and I didn't see the neighborhood's ecology because we'd never visualized Thousand Oaks in predominantly ecological terms. We might describe the content of Fig. 22, for example, as a scattering of leaves waiting to be raked up or blown away. For Fig. 23, visible and esthetic contrasts might be paramount.

Fig. 21. Accurate but Unrepresentative Photos.
These two photographs are objectively accurate but highly unrepresentative of how the neighborhood "usually looks." *Source:* Photos by Jon Wagner.

Evidence of the Thousand Oaks ecological community, however, was continuously and clearly visible to anyone who looked for it – anyone, that is, who looked as thoughtfully as Gary Snyder (1990) or Jenny Odell (2019). And from that perspective, the photos in Figs. 22 and 23 could be read in ecological terms such as those appearing in the captions I've provided.

Captions for photographs can provide useful information, but they also embed images in larger narratives. For most images appearing in this essay, the implicit narrative of the captions assigns human residents a leading role. We could do that for Fig. 24, for example, by noting that, "To the East, Thousand Oaks extends into the Berkeley Hills where the winding streets and an uneven topology make parking cars a greater challenge and encounters with deer more common." The caption for Fig. 24 reflects a more ecologically attuned perspective.

The narratives we apply to images may be works of our imagination, but that doesn't mean they lack consequences. In Thousand Oaks and other neighborhoods, for example, it's worth knowing that every material object visible in the photos throughout this essay – whether or not it's alive – exists within and helps define an ecological community. This "natural" community is linked, in turn, to neighboring locales and the larger region in ways that shape the fate of local and regional species and their habitats. Every organism or machine that moves or

Fig. 22.   Falling Leaves as an Ecological Event.
When deciduous trees replace their solar collectors every year, they voluntarily withhold water and food. This dehydrates and weakens collector-to-tree bonds so that, eventually, even a gentle breeze will release a collector from its host tree so it can fall to the ground. In urban areas, many collectors are then raked into piles by human beings, loaded into plastic bags and transported to remote dumping grounds. Left where they fall, however, spent collectors such as these will shelter insects, bacteria, molds and microorganisms that transform them into forms that nourish and sustain other living things. *Source:* Photo by Jon Wagner.

grows within this community also consumes energy and contributes positively or negatively to the carbon footprint of the neighborhood and the oxygen resources available to human beings and other air-breathing residents.

We can think about the implicit narratives that frame how we see images of neighborhoods as a form of "alignment." This term captures both the visual act of seeing things "in a line" and the conceptual act of linking one thing to another. Lining things up visually that we might otherwise consider unrelated, for example, can prompt us to think more about visual/physical connections to the natural world that our social life and aspirations frequently neglect, trivialize, or deny.

That's true as well for "lining up" the materials and practices we live with and their consequences for the environment we live within. Those alignments underscore the seriousness of relationships between human beings and other

Fig. 23.   Visual and Ecological Design.
On the right, landscaping adjacent front yards as a common area with drought
resistant plants visually erases a property line and allows rain water to sink into the
earth and benefit the local the water table. On the left, the concrete pavement and
double fence emphasize the property line and direct rain water into a storm sewer. The
residents of all four homes can probably tell stories about their landscape treatments,
and the stories would likely reflect personal truths that they live with – only a few of
which might acknowledge the ecological community they live within. *Source:* Photos
by Jon Wagner.

organisms living in roughly the same space, their joint entanglements in matters
of life and death, and their impact on the future of where they live. As characterized by Yuval Noah Harari (see Marchese, 2021), it seems at times as if our
knowledge about these relationships has outpaced our narratives of how to live
with them harmoniously.

10. RESIDENT MATERIALS, VISIBILITY, AND AGENCY

My understanding of what the visual commons entailed emerged from what
residents said about where they lived, what they noticed, and what they seemed to
care about. Rather late in the game, it dawned on me that residents were engaged
as much or more with materials and objects they could arrange and display to
others as they were with what I'd noted as the area's visibly dominant features.

Getting rid of rubbish and trash, for example, involved city-mandated routines
that engaged residents in the weekly ritual of separating their refuse into four bins
– for composting, paper recycling, metal and plastic recycling, or landfill – and

Fig. 24.   A Multi-species Ecological Community.
In the background of this photo can be seen fragments of several houses and fences
and a grove of varied, largely self-sustaining shrubs and trees that extend across
property lines, the city owned easement strip and individual parcels of privately
owned land. In the foreground, two species of community residents, each appearing
in this moment as passersby to the other, make their way past a line of automobiles,
each of which is privately owned (or leased) by an individual person or two and
stationed, at least temporarily, on city-owned streets. *Source:* Photo by Jon Wagner.

placing the bins on the street in time for collection by the city's waste management service. Local ordinances forbid placing bins on the street prior to trash
pick-up day and mandated that they be returned to a householder's property by
the end of that day. It fell on residents to enact their side of this routine and on
the city to enact its part. Observed irregularities on either side prompted comments among neighbors or between residents and the city (Fig. 25).

Trash bins were not the only visible materials residents moved in and out of
view in Thousand Oaks. Many residents also temporarily used driveways, parts
of their front or side yards, easement strips, or the street itself as staging areas for
materials they received (building and landscaping supplies, large appliances, and
automobile repair projects) or planned to deliver elsewhere (large tree pruning,
home demolition debris, discarded carpet, and cardboard boxes). Courting
ambiguities that might perplex outsiders, residents use the same areas to display
materials set out as donations for their neighbors or passersby. Householders
typically trust other residents to figure out what is trash, open storage or free to
take, but they sometimes include signs to clarify – e.g., "Lemons FREE. box is
NOT!" (See also the two bottom photos in Fig. 7) (Fig. 26).

Fig. 25.   Setting for Trash Day Performance.
Props are in place for a weekly "trash day" performance by residents and the city's
waste management service. Green bins are for green debris, divided blue bins for
paper (brown lid side) and plastics/metal (blue lid side), and grey bins for landfill.
Source: Photos by Jon Wagner.

Conspicuous and imaginative use of visible materials also appears in resident
landscaping, decorating, home maintenance, and remodeling activities. For the
area as a whole, these generate a continuous stream of visible activities and
changes. Trees are pruned, fences and windows painted, lawns and shrubs
trimmed and watered, a house extended from one story to two or a garage
converted to living space, and so on. Above and beyond household maintenance,
many residents decorate their street side yards, homes, windows, and trees to
visibly recognize holidays (Halloween and Christmas, in particular) or express
social or political ideals.

Displaying signs, posters, and flags; or arranging stones, tiles, gravel, and
plants; or adding physical features to their homes and yard all require time,
attention, and other resources. Resident responses to changes their neighbors
make are frequently mixed about particulars. Taken together, however, they
reflect a shared interest in how the neighborhood looks. Chatter and stories about
who's doing what also confirm for residents that their landscaping and decorating
efforts are noticed by an audience of their peers (Fig. 27).

Efforts by Thousand Oaks residents to manage and display materials in and
around their household and yard are an expressive counterpart to looking
actively at where they live. In working with materials they can acquire, manip-
ulate, control, and display according to their own likes and dislikes, residents
exercise a kind of individual agency that is personally meaningful and publicly

Fig. 26. Resident Donations and Storage.
Residents set out materials on sidewalks, driveways, easement strips or their own front yards as donations, trash, temporary storage or decorations. Residents sometimes assume that passersby can judge which of these categories apply, but frequently provide signs to clarify. Castoff books are something of a special case. They're passed on through the numerous mini "lending libraries" that dot the area (as in the photo bottom left) but are also offered up simply by being displayed street side on tables (as in the photo bottom right), in boxes or even on the sidewalk itself.
Source: Photos by Jon Wagner.

Fig. 27.   Resident Decorations and Embellishments.
Residents use a rich array of acquired and arranged materials (including plantings and
paintings) to decorate, embellish, and add visual distinction to their homes and yards.
At least some of these also engage the interest of their neighbors and other passersby.
Source: Photos by Jon Wagner.

recognized. This agency falls short of what it would take to alter visibly dominant features of the neighborhood – pavement, cars, houses, and large trees – but it's strong enough to elicit from residents a shared sense of ownership for how "their" neighborhood looks.

11. THE VISUAL COMMONS AS A NEIGHBORHOOD WORKSPACE

In this essay, I've tried to illustrate how residents of Thousand Oaks engage with each other about visible features of where they live. This engagement with what they can see, or imagine seeing, vitalizes neighborhood life in ways that can pull residents closer together or farther apart. Agreements about how where they live looks or should look can help residents to feel they are living together in the same neighborhood, and disagreements can have the opposite effect. But even disagreements offer participants a shared experience of caring about how their neighborhood looks.

Does this shared attention to how things look generate among Thousand Oaks residents a sense of community? By itself, probably not, at least not for the full-featured communities idealized by Keller and other community scholars. But it does seem to nourish, through what I'm calling a visual commons, the collective engagement of residents in where they live. So, what does this commons entail? How have residents brought it into being? And where is it located?

A Collection of Cognitive Maps? I initially thought of the visual commons as overlapping areas of individual resident's cognitive maps. The concept of a "cognitive map" can be useful in affirming that residents not only develop individual visualizations of where they live, but, in some sense, live within those visualizations, not just in what outsiders might regard as "the place itself."

In contrast to standard issue maps and diagrams, however, resident visualizations are multidimensional, situational, and dynamic. They're more akin to an ever-changing audiovisual reference manual (or visual wiki) that can generate a memory constellation of what residents have seen and heard and said and done, over time and in association with other people, neighborhood features, social settings, and the lore of personal and neighborhood stories. Two-dimensional diagrams of boundaries and paths and a few notable physical features are not a good metaphor for that, let alone an accurate depiction. So maps may not be the best foundation for grounding a concept like the visual commons.

A Collective Perspective? Another potential candidate for conceptualizing a visual commons is the kind of "perspective" that Becker et al. (1961) placed at the theoretical center of their study of medical schools students. Two aspects of that align closely with what I've been exploring in Thousand Oaks. First, the "perspectives" featured in that study help individuals make sense of something they can't otherwise understand. In the authors' words, "A person develops and maintains a perspective when he faces a situation calling for action which is not given by his own prior beliefs or by situational imperatives" (Becker et al., 1961, p. 35). Second, common elements of individual perspectives can be regarded as a "collective perspective" that orients a person toward problematic situations that multiple individuals face together.

The visual commons could be regarded as a collective perspective in which how things look in the neighborhood and the visualizations of other residents are highly valued. Flowing into this shared perspective would be residents' individual visualizations of where they live. Flowing out would be a sense of how other residents see where they live and a shared appreciation for the importance of how things look. But what might prompt neighborhood residents to develop a collective "visual" perspective of this sort?

That question initially stumped me. But over time, I began to notice all the ways in which the existential fact of living in the same area with other people over whom they have little or no control might stimulate residents to develop a collective perspective, especially – as Suttles (1968) noted for the neighborhoods he studied – if people want or need to trust or be trusted by other residents. As a framework for articulating ideas and action, a "perspective" could also direct a resident's attention to visible and visual elements. But in Thousand Oaks, visual elements themselves seemed to be the framework for linking ideas and actions, not the other way around, and I didn't want to lose that.

A Network of Social Relationships? Theoretical concepts can fall short of what we'd like, but still give us something useful to think about, and that's no doubt true for cognitive maps and collective perspectives. But, if both concepts miss something essential about the visual commons, why not just focus on "social relationships" between residents? We could say, for example, that, "Thousand Oaks residents develop social connections with each other that include opportunities to share how things look where they live." This statement certainly does ring true. But social networks for Thousand Oaks residents extend far beyond the neighborhood in which they live. And a lot goes on among residents about how things look in Thousand Oaks that the term "social relationships" don't come close to capturing.

Worldmaking? Nelson Goodman's concept of "worldmaking" (1978) does a better job than the other three in capturing process dimensions of the visual commons. As I noted earlier, it's also a useful term for characterizing how Thousand Oaks residents develop visualizations of where they live. In both contexts, social, cognitive, and creative work can take the form of composition and decomposition, weighting different levels of relevance, ordering, and so – all of which Goodman examines as aspects of worldmaking.

There's also plenty of room within Goodman's notions about worldmaking for residents to blend material realities, imaginative projections, speculations, and fantasies into visualizations of their neighborhood. Yet another parallel is a recursive relationship between creating, knowing, and the truth. As Goodman puts it, "Discovering laws involves drafting them. Recognizing patterns is very much a matter of inventing and imposing them. Comprehension and creation go on together" (1978, p. 22). On the other hand, worldmaking provides no obvious hooks for identifying visible dimensions of a neighborhood as a primary interface for collective engagement.

Each of these four concepts corresponds in part to what I've called the "visual commons," and each offers insights into how residents experience living in Thousand Oaks. So, then, why not consider all four? And why not treat them as multiple, defining features and dimensions of the visual commons? Fair enough, but what then does the concept of a visual commons add that's not provided by the dimensions themselves?

This last question led me to a key feature of neighborhood life that's missing not only from each of the other four concepts but also from community studies in general: the symbolic "place" or "space" where residents can develop a collective perspective, share their common material circumstances and their visualizations of where they live, engage in local worldmaking, and vitalize their relationships with each other. This missing feature, I realized, is framed as a negative space by the other four dimensions. And, functionally, it's the otherwise implicit link between neighbors and the process of forming neighborly relationships. That is, in much the same way that a friendship (or family, organization, or polity) is the context in which people develop and share a friendship (or family, organization or polity), the visual commons is the context in which residents develop and share their common engagement with visible features of where they live.

The visual commons exists, then – in both resident imaginations and social interaction – as a kind of workspace. It's a concept, embodied in the behavior of residents, for sharing how they see where they live and visualizing how they want that to look. It's also a process through which residents fashion, out of their visualizations a place where they can see themselves as, and become, neighbors. And it's a product of ongoing exchanges, both real and imagined, in which residents affirm the importance of how things look where they live, share visualizations of what they see and would like to see, and recognize, as neighbors, others who see some of the same things (Fig. 28).

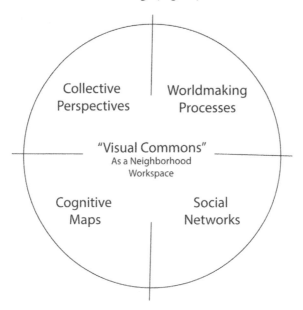

Fig. 28. The Visual Commons as Negative Space and Workspace.

Seen in this way, the visual commons is not a defining feature of the ideal typical "community" described by Keller (2003), but it might be a defining feature of what we think of as a "neighborhood." At the very least, it's a reminder that communitarian sensibilities, broadly defined, can serve both individual and collective interests when people live in circumstances that they visualize as a shared space.

As an extension of that reminder, the visual commons is also an intriguing way to think about nonplace "neighborhoods" supported through audio and visual media. When we engage with other people over whom we have little or no control in any kind of shared, visible environment – even what we now refer to as "virtual" – we might find ourselves exploring something similar to a visual commons. At the most elemental level, this could involve affirming the importance of how things look. Beyond that, it might also be reflected in our curiosity about how others see the same place, how well their visualizations correspond to our own, and what materials we're provided with to make even a nonplace place look more like we want it to look.

The same combination of cognitive mapping, perspective sharing, and worldmaking could be set in motion even among people who recognize – in satellite photographs of its shrinking ice caps – the earth as a global "neighborhood" we share. It might emerge also among people who follow a news story or research development, at least some of whom desire to share what they see, and would like to see, in and around where they and other "followers" are engaged. In these and other instances, wanting a neighborhood where we are living to look the way we want it to look reflects, at least in part, the world in which we are trying to live and with whom.

12. BEYOND THOUSAND OAKS

What can we say about Thousand Oaks that might apply to other residential areas? Certainly not that trees and shrubs and single-family homes are visibly dominant, nor that raccoons, crows, and bougainvillea are well represented among local flora and fauna. The demographics are in no way universal either, nor are property taxes or proximity to an annual street fair.

On the other hand, the residents of any populated local area face challenges that come from living nearby other people over whom they have little, if any, control (Suttles, 1968, p. 233). With that in mind, as both species members and persons, people living in radically different neighborhoods might similarly value opportunities to present themselves to other residents – in person and through arranged materials – in ways that can potentially affirm who they are and where they live. That could engage residents of neighborhoods quite different from Thousand Oaks in some version of a visual commons. If so, to understand how people are living nearby each other – perhaps anywhere – it would be useful to know how they visualize where they live and the challenges that present for them.

This essay has hopefully suggested and illustrated some ways of exploring those kinds of visualizations. Writing it has also led me to embrace two ideas about neighborhood and community life that I had not previously considered. The first follows from the extension I noted earlier from Goffman's work (Goffman, 1961, p.

180) – i.e., that every description of a neighborhood implicitly includes a conception of its residents. The second follows from what I came to feel about where I live.

In terms of the first idea, three different versions of this relationship strike me as noteworthy ways of describing a neighborhood: as a group of human beings living in roughly the same area; as a population of sociocultural persons sharing a collective living space; and as a constellation of ecological actors and agents living among other actors and agents, each contributing to the life and order of the physical environment they share (Fig. 29).

Prior to writing this essay, I had not considered this triad of perspectives on neighborhood and community life. And it was only after doing so that I fully recognized how visual studies can contribute to all three, either serially or simultaneously. To investigate "human beings," for example, traditional forms of direct observation, audiovisual analysis and natural experiments (such as those practiced by ethologists) are good bets. For "socio-cultural persons," participant observation and photo- or video-elicitation interviews may be valuable, or even necessary. To study a range of "ecological actors," direct observations and audiovisual analysis can be expanded from *Homo sapiens* to include other species.

The second idea I'm now living with as a result of writing this essay has to do with the depth of what we don't know about how neighborhoods, settlements, and communities intersect within individual lives. The homes we locate in neighborhoods to house social persons are also shelters for species members, and,

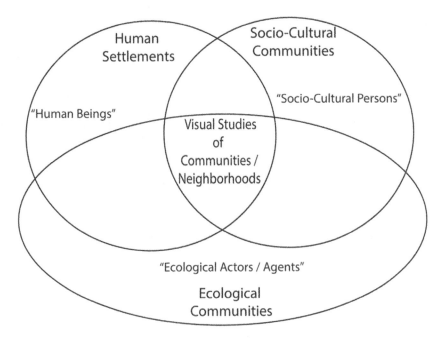

Fig. 29. Neighborhoods, Communities, and Members: Three Overlapping Conceptions.

Fig. 30.   The Thousand Oaks Neighborhood.

This street level view of Thousand Oaks is looking down from the top of the same street that appears in Fig. 1. In both directions, the visible neighborhood includes a street lined with cars and telephone poles and a mass of trees and bushes within which we can see fragments of the homes, in and around which, residents are living their lives. *Source:* Photo by Jon Wagner.

ecologically speaking, machines for generating or consuming energy and for sustaining and depleting different life forms. As social persons, our days may be oriented toward tasks and pastimes, but as species members they're also an exercise of survival skills, and as ecological actors they contribute to local and regional developments that make some futures more likely than others.

After writing this essay, I'm not only wondering how these multiple perspectives intersect with the lives we live, I'm also on the prowl for images and stories that could help us think about that. I'm also wondering how we could learn to look more closely – not just at how and where we live but also at how and where we look! Beyond that, it seems worthwhile to explore strategies for visualizing where we've been and might be heading next, not just as individual residents but also as neighbors (Fig. 30).

REFERENCES

Alexievich, S. (2006/1997). *Voices from Chernobyl: The oral history of a nuclear disaster.* New York, NY: Picador.

Becker, H. S., Geer, B., Hughes, E. C., & Strauss, A. L. (1961/1977). *Boys in white: Student culture in medical school.* Piscataway, NJ: Transaction Publishers.

Doheny-Farina, S. (1996). *The wired neighborhood.* New Haven, CT: Yale University Press.

Goffman, E. (1961). *Asylums: Essays on the social situation of mental patients and other inmates.* Garden City, NY: Anchor Books.

Goodman, N. (1978). *Ways of worldmaking.* Indianapolis, IN: Hackett.

Keller, S. (1976). *Twin Rivers: Study of a planned community.* Washington, DC: National Technical Information Service (NSF/RA-760749).

Keller, S. (2003). *Community: Pursuing the dream, living the reality.* Princeton, NJ: Princeton University Press.

Lynch, K. (1960). *The image of a city.* Cambridge, MA: M.I.T. Press.

Marchese, D. (2021). Yuvel Noah Harari believes this simple story can save the planet. *New York Times Magazine.* November 7, 2021.

Myerhoff, B. (1978). *Number our days.* New York, NY: Simon and Schuster/Touchstone.

Odell, J. (2019). *How to do nothing: Resisting the attention economy.* Brooklyn, NY: Melville House.

Seuss, Dr. (1958). *Yertle the Turtle and other stories.* New York, NY: Random House.

Snyder, G. (1990). *The practice of the wild.* Berkeley, CA: Counterpoint.

Suchar, C. S. (1997). Grounding visual sociology research in shooting scripts. *Qualitative Sociology, 20*(1), 33–55.

Suttles, G. D. (1968). *The social order of the slum: Ethnicity and territory in the inner city.* Chicago, IL: University of Chicago Press.

Suttles, G. D. (1972). *The social construction of communities.* Chicago, IL: University of Chicago Press.

Terkel, S. (2006). *Division street: America.* New York, NY: The New Press.

Wagner, J. (1979a). Perceiving a planned community. In J. Wagner (Ed.), *Images of information: Still photography in social science teaching and research* (pp. 69–84). Beverly Hills, CA: SAGE Publication.

Wagner, J. (1979b). Avoiding error. In J. Wagner (Ed.), *Images of information: Still photography in social science teaching and research* (pp. 147–160). Beverly Hills, CA: SAGE Publication.

Wagner, J. (2014). Lot lines and tree falls: Exploring the visual commons in an upscale community. Paper presented at *the annual meetings of the International Visual Sociology Association,* Pittsburgh, PA, June 2014. Duquesne University.

Wagner, J. (2016). Fieldwork, archives and photographic materials. In K. Zeleny (Ed.), *Materialities: Pocket essays 01.* Berlin: The Velvet Cell.

Chapter 4

BURNED OUT: A VISUAL AND LYRICAL SOCIOLOGY OF SMOKING IN THE CITY

Stephen Coleman and Jim Brogden

ABSTRACT

This chapter explores a common, but typically overlooked urban practice: smoking outside the workplace. This activity is analysed as an attempt to create marginal spaces of brief retreat from the acceleration and agitation of the workplace. By talking to smokers about what drives them into the street, and capturing smokers photographically, we discover that these people are seeking moments of breakaway from the dominating involvement of the commercial city. The practices we observe in this chapter are typical of what Erving Goffman refers to as 'away' activities: strategies for briefly escaping from the absorption of all-consuming social situations. We conclude by asking whether these urban pauses could be stretched to a point where they challenge the compulsion of the overwrought rhythmic order of the capitalist city.

Keywords: Smoking; workplace; street; pause; involvement; Goffman

1. INTRODUCTION

What are they doing, these men and women who gather in the shadows of tall towers to inhale and then exhale distractedly? We kept running into them as we ambled around the city in search of those pulsating offbeats that disturb its illusive orderliness; those moments of respite that quietly belie the frenetic urban rhythm. First, we saw the tall towers, buzzing with a nervous commercial exuberance, like relentless mechanisms in search of an intelligible purpose. Surrounding them were sandwich bars performing bad auditions as Mediterranean

Visual and Multimodal Urban Sociology, Part B
Research in Urban Sociology, Volume 18B, 103–123
Copyright © 2023 by Emerald Publishing Limited
ISSN: 1047-0042/doi:10.1108/S1047-00422023000018B004

street cafes; multi-storey car parks, discreetly stacking away the means of speedy return to personal space; and a dizzying array of hieroglyphic logos, ads, street signs and graffiti. We were semiotically as well as geographically in the centre of a big post-industrial city.[1] Unsure what we were seeing or even what we were looking for, we kept returning to the city centre and focusing on the same peripheral scene.

They gathered near the entrances to the office towers, sometimes in thinly sociable clusters, but more often alone, puffing, sucking in, blowing out and vigorously respiring, as if enacting a quiet toxic ritual. Over time, their compulsion became ours. The more often we observed it, the more opaque this urban sideshow seemed to be. Typically registered through a sort of peripheral urban vision, this arcane social practice appeared to be saying something about the late-modern city. But what?

Focusing upon the detail, here were individuals returning repeatedly to the scene of a never quite completed performance. They would emerge from the buildings, light up and briefly linger. Some paced. Some looked hopefully at their phones. Some exchanged words. Nothing much ever happened. When they left their spot by the entrance there was no trace of them having been there. It was a hit and run without the drama of a collision. The effect of the scene lay in its indistinct ephemerality.

It eventually became clear to us that focusing upon the details of this scene was misleading. It was like staring at a feature at the extreme edge of a Brueghel painting, hoping that it might illuminate an encompassing meaning. Step back from the fugitive figure of the smokers and the wider canvas begins to offer its clues. That wider canvas is the city, not so much as a place on a map or in empirical motion, but as a confluence of pressing, cramming, overwhelming activities. Cities are hubs of over-activity, overloading their socialised inhabitants with occupational and sensory stimuli that drive them, quite literally, to distraction. As Simmel (1964 [1903], p. 410) put it, 'The psychological basis of the metropolitan type of individuality consists in the intensification of nervous stimulation which results from the swift and uninterrupted change of outer and inner stimuli'. The default atmosphere of cities, suggested Stanley Milgram (1970, p. 1462), is one of neural overload:

> City life, as we experience it, constitutes a continuous set of encounters with overload, and of resultant adaptations. Overload characteristically deforms daily life on several levels, impinging on role performance, the evolution of social norms, cognitive functioning, and the use of facilities.

Contemporary urban geographers have turned their attention to the atmospherics of city living, offering astute analyses of what it means to be caught up within a neuroarchitecture that induces permanent stress (Fitzgerald, Rose, & Singh, 2016; Gandy, 2020; Pykett, Osborne, & Resch, 2020). As accounts emerge

---

[1]The city was Leeds, the fifth largest city in the United Kingdom. It comprises an area of 42 square miles (109 square kilometres), with a population of 443,247. Most of our research was conducted within the city centre; see Fig. 1.

of how places can not only engender subjective feeling but also flatten the scope for affective resonance (Navaro-Yashin, 2009), it begins to become apparent how the terms of everyday urban survival are vulnerable to framing forms of atmospheric acceleration, abjection and agitation. As Walter Benjamin was always eager to point out, the construction of the overwrought, hyperactive city is built upon the destruction of gentler customs of human intercourse.

Nowhere is this more apparent than in the contemporary urban office, where people are confronted by pressures to perform 'flexibly'; to adapt to hyperactive processes and imperative deadlines; to engage with multiple, competing networks of communication and association; to pursue competitive strategies of career advancement, while all the while maintaining affective displays appropriate to conditions of hierarchical control and worktime intimacy. Overwhelmed by these ever-intensifying demands, many urban workers find themselves fluctuating between nervous over-excitement and languid debilitation. Burned out by the city, they look for escape routes.

The desire to flee and recover, if only for brief moments, reminds urban office workers that they possess personal agency, however constrained that might be. 'Breaking up the day', as several of our interviewees referred to their brief retreats from the workplace, becomes an act of resistance to being broken up by the day. Much has been written by sociologists of work about the function and value of work breaks. John Trougakos and Ivona Hideg (2009, p. 45) note that 'in order to recover from the negative effects of work, people need to have work breaks', but that 'simply taking a break may not be enough':

> What seems to be important is how people use their breaks. More specifically, it seems that in order to recover, people need to use their break time to engage in activities that stop the demands associated with work ... Thus, in order to recover, people must use their breaks to engage in respite activities. We define respite activities as break activities that involve either low effort or preferred choice.

Breaking from the intensive pace of work involves more than simply jumping off the metaphorical treadmill. In Goffmanesque terms, the emotional value of work breaks lies in a transition from front-stage role performance, be it as a specific kind of worker or a more generalised city dweller, into a backstage region in which the choking responsibilities of role maintenance can be relaxed or even abandoned. Work breaks take people into liminal spaces where 'anything may happen' (Turner, 1974). These are temporary spaces, such as entrances to buildings, which are neither obviously inside or outside; private or public; for recharging or winding down. They are pockets of counterfactual possibility that crop up within and against the city, defying its relentless rhythm through a form of subversion in plain sight.

When you look closely at a city, marginal spaces of brief retreat begin to become apparent. The smokers and vapers who gather outside urban buildings regularly enter such ad hoc zones in which everything that constitutes the buzz and bustle, restlessness and transience, and sensory encumbrance of urban life is briefly suspended. Scope for extrication and relief is integral to the urban imaginary. The nineteenth-century creation of urban parks, which were seen as the 'lungs of the city', was largely motivated by utilitarian instincts (Crompton, 2013), but there was also the influence of what we might call the utopian unconscious whereby parks were seen as spaces in which the city could be cast off, while never actually left. Informal smoking areas reflect a similar urban counter-arrangement. They are spaces in which people can feel free to indulge in what the city routinely denies them: alone time; room to breathe; purposeless activity.

As we became more curious to understand the individuals and small groups who gathered outside city buildings, seemingly regardless of the weather, we began to wonder just how much the cigarettes and vapes that they smoked told us about the practice that they were engaged in. It was tempting to see these people as addicts (Eiser, Sutton, & Wober, 1977) or exiles (Fedele & Borland, 1998), forced out on to the cold pavements by tenacious compulsions and regulative bans, but was that really what was going on? Brief, informal conversations with smokers we accosted on the street suggested a more complex story. We resolved to dig deeper, pursuing our investigation in two closely related ways.

Firstly, we conducted in-depth interviews with people who regularly leave their workplace to smoke or vape. It was remarkable how quickly these interviews moved beyond a focus upon the act of smoking. Just as attempts to understand why people visit pubs are unlikely to be realised by focusing upon the content of beer mugs or capturing experiences of voting is likely to result from detailed questioning about the act of putting a pencil cross on an official form, when our interviewees were asked to reflect upon why they go outside to smoke, their relationship to cigarettes was rarely central to the narrative. Much more important to the people we spoke to was the act of going outside; the episodic value that they derived from the break. Our curiosity was driven by a desire to understand what exactly was being broken away from during these moments of escape. As the historians, Trentmann and Normal (2009, pp. 68–69) point out, breakdowns 'open up the temporal fragility of habits and the elasticity of everyday life':

> They offer a snapshot of rhythms as they unravel and are braided back together again, capturing the work that is needed to keep them going. Disruptions, in this view, are not freak accidents or aberrations but natural, constitutive features of lived normality.

Much of what emerged from the interviews suggests that smokers are searching for moments of hiatus in which they are briefly released from an exhausting rhythm. By exploring the nature of that urban throb and the experience of relief from it we gain a valuable insight into the ways in which cities quite literally drive people to distraction.

Personal testimony tells part of the story, but only that which can be recalled after the event. Our second method of investigation involved observation of these episodes as they were happening. The photographic evidence was produced with a view to celebrating the individuality of each smoker as a unique urban protagonist, whilst recognising that their presence and performance in the urban landscape might resonate beyond their specific urban location.

Importantly, we sought to adopt a respectful distance from our subjects so as to preclude the voyeuristic aspect associated with some forms of street photography. It was important to eschew an 'in-your-face' method, recognisable in the street photography of Garry Winogrand and Vivian Maier. In fact, we would argue, that because the public is increasingly aware of photographic practice and issues of personal privacy, compounded by its rapid dissemination through social media, it is almost untenable to operate as a 'traditional' street photographer, even though it is not illegal to photograph in public space.

The places in which smokers decided to stand were important too. In some sense, their choice of location indicated a subtle disturbance to the pedestrian flow of the city. In this photographic approach, we reflected upon the choices that smokers made about which space to occupy. Were these places of safety – or belonging – or vantage points for observing the city? As we cast our ethnographic eye on them, what were they casting theirs upon? We began to wonder whether the cigarettes were decoys, allowing people to witness and track the city as lay ethnographers. As we conducted our research, we began to feel immersed in a dynamic of urban panoptic surveillance: us watching them watching others watching each other. It was time to move closer.

2. TALKING TO SMOKERS

Before turning to the interviews, in which we employed the most obvious strategy of research – asking smokers what they thought they were doing – it is worth focusing for a moment upon the interview situation itself. An interview is an encounter in which there is a commitment by two or more people to perform themselves to one another. The distinctive challenges of this joint performance involve demanding work. The interviewer engages in attempts to frame the situation; build mutual trust; direct the flow of conversation and show that she is able to listen, understand and avoid judgemental responses. The interviewee endeavours to present a consistent and comprehensible self; relate experiences, feelings, knowledge and values in a narratively meaningful fashion and 'work constantly to discern and designate the recognizable and orderly features of the experience under consideration' (Gubrium & Holstein, 2002, p. 14). Within the interview situation much energy is devoted to leaning forward, sitting back, gesturing, turn-taking signals, emotional displays and efforts to contain hesitations and silences. It is interesting to watch people as they leave an interview. Their participatory obligations are over. The demands upon their attention are lifted. They are no longer involved in, but away from the situation. As we watched people leave the scene of the interview we had an insight into a fundamental need: the chance to remove oneself from that which was previously all-absorbing. Of course, we hoped that our interviews with smokers were not so onerous that getting away would feel like a blessed release, but that was the story that most of them told us about getting away from their workplaces.

As spaces of institutionalised hyper-activity, late-modern urban workplaces not only consume the attention of their hired participants within their incessant and simultaneous streams of communicative connection and obligations to multi-task but also are draining frontstage arenas within which an unceasing performance of self must be kept up. Workers are not only expected to labour for long hours at an accelerated pace but also to 'do being a worker' over and over again every hour of every day. Much has been written about the toll taken by this combination of physical and emotional labour and the need to periodically press the pause button.

Robert Snow and Dennis Brissett's (1986) exploration of 'pausing' offers a valuable theoretical insight into the meaning of such breaks in the routine flow of the daily grind. They point out that pauses should not be understood in terms of what people have stopped doing, but as social acts in their own right. Pauses, as 'individualised departures from the concerted task at hand', are not moments of inaction but of non-interaction in an obligatory social rhythm. In *Behaviour in Public Places*, Goffman (1963, p. 43) distinguishes between the calls of 'involvement', in which people must adapt themselves to the speed, intensity, mood and rhythms of the interaction order and being 'away', which refers to withdrawal from such demands – ruminative and recuperative periods of inattention. As Goffman (1961, p. 320) put it with characteristic metaphorical elegance:

> Our sense of being a person can come from being drawn into a wider social unit; our sense of selfhood can arise through the little ways in which we resist the pull. Our status is backed by the solid buildings of the world, while our sense of personal identity often resides in the cracks.

It was to the cracks that our interviewees led us. Asked why they went outside to smoke, the desire for pause was typically the first and most emphatic explanation that they offered us. Karen, a hospital administrator in a highly pressurised work environment, explained that:

> It is literally a five-minute break from everything for me ... It's an escape, I think, from the daily grind.

We asked her whether she had to be smoking a cigarette for this escape to be accomplished. At first, she found it difficult to separate the two acts, but then she said,

> To be fair, it doesn't even have to be smoking. It's just leaving the office ... But obviously, my habit is smoking, that's just an excuse for leaving the office. Because if I didn't smoke, I'd end up getting sucked into something else like taking a phone call or ...

Patty, who was working at home during the pandemic lockdown, told us how she still went outside the back door of her house several times a day to smoke a cigarette. She described this as 'having a pause in my work' and went on to explain:

> So, I'm likely to go for one after a video meeting or something. I'm likely to think 'Right, I just need to get out of this room'.

Patty is in her own home, temporarily repurposed as a domestic office place. She is not tied into a surrounding labour regime. She is not forced outside by a smoking ban. So why go outside?

> I'm someone with quite a lot of nervous energy. I don't tend to do nothing. I'm always like doing something. If I wasn't having a cigarette, I'd be on my phone checking Twitter or something ... I don't feel I could have a pause without the cigarette. But I have been smoking since I was a teenager. And I'm 35 now, so ...

For Patty, smoking breaks are not moments of 'doing nothing', but an attempt to manage her own attention. She tells us that 'It's something I can just do on auto-pilot almost'.

When Janice spoke about smoking breaks she seemed to ascribe to them an agency of their own, as if they were giving something to her:

> It's making me go outside. It's making me stop. It's making me move away from my desk and my office for five to ten minutes. It's actually removing me from the situation ... I suppose it forces you to have a break.

For Janice, the break is not an outcome in itself, but a trigger for reconnecting with her own bodily rhythm. The cigarette becomes a heroic figure, saving her from what might otherwise feel ineludible.

Willie has ADHD and feels that smoking breaks help him to cope with it:

> I've got a propensity to use things that distract me. So, it's definitely that ... it's a rewarding thing, you know ... It's like 'I need to get away'. I need the cigarette to release me from the situation.

We asked him how he would feel if he were not allowed to leave his workspace to smoke:

> I would be upset. It would be like losing a little moment in my day. It's all I ask for. I mean, I work my arse off. Like, can I just have this one little thing?

Like Willie, Leroy feels that he needs smoking breaks to relieve his stress:

> I use it to calm myself down. I've got quite high anxiety generally as a person, so I find that those ten minutes every now and again, they give me a bit of peace, a bit of time for myself to just zen out, kind of.

Harry works in a large open-plan office in a multi-storey building and told us that smoking breaks are quite simply 'an excuse to get away from my desk'. But he has no illusion about the ephemerality of these small pauses:

> Obviously, in the five minutes you get to be out of the office you smoke and maybe have a chat, you're not thinking about your work. But as soon as you're finished you're straight back in.

Whatever leaving the workplace to smoke might have to do with feeding an addiction, it is, regardless of that, a pause from a besieging rhythm. Smoking breaks are short periods of reprieve, but are not just empty interruptions, moments of vacuous withdrawal. They are functional. People use these times to do something that is not part of their work but is part of their lives. There were four main purposes that our interviewees ascribed to smoking breaks. In practice, these are not mutually exclusive and may not be exhaustive of the various ways in which workers use such breaks. Our aim was to help interviewees describe the texture and feeling of these functions; to learn from them how pausing opens up space in the city for experiences that the work rhythm ignores or smothers.

The first way in which smoking breaks are used is for reflection. In theory, thinking and doing are closely linked. In the context of the hyper-accelerated workplace, pressure to do without prior or reflective thought is inescapable. Much of what happens at work cannot be adequately processed. People find themselves caught up in institutional routines and excited surges of activity in which reflection is regarded as an extravagance. As for non-work matters, reflection is implicitly regarded as an incursion into bought time. One is not paid to think about personal concerns. But can people survive for days on end without such retreats into reflection on their work or personal lives?

Janice explained that:

> It takes me away from the process. It's a time to gather my own thoughts and then return ... It's almost like a reset, going out of the building and gathering your thoughts and then deciding what to do next.

Similarly, Karen told us that:

> It just give you five minutes maybe for a bit of reflection ... Mentally, you need that break. Ironically, I work in the cancer team and I smoke. It's just so fast paced. You just need that five minutes of headspace.

We asked Karen to describe this mental lull. She said that usually it involved quiet retracing of things that have happened; time to weigh up decisions made and pending. But sometimes she leaves her office together with a colleague:

> We're usually yacking and having a whinge and it's probably a good time to vent about stuff that's happened at work. Just have a good vent and come back in, happier usually.

Some interviewees wanted to explain that these pauses were more than just skiving opportunities. Time to reflect, they suggested, was essential to their mental wellbeing:

> I'll probably reflect on situations that happen during the day. It really is a stress relief. (Leroy)

> I know it's not a healthy habit, but ... me personally as a smoker, I would say that there are benefits from going outside and smoking. Not health benefits, but other benefits. Social benefits. Even mental benefits ... (Harry)

This led to a second, closely related function of smoking breaks – one that surprised us. Several people told us that these were moments of meditation. More than just casual reflection, they regarded these breaks as opportunities for brief but deep spiritual repair. Karen explained that:

> I say it's crucial. It's almost like a form of meditation where you can have a little break from the world ... It almost brings a private space to me, if that makes sense. In a busy state, with a lot of things around you, it brings a bit of tranquillity.

Patty compared smoking breaks with other forms of relief from stress:

> If I wanted a longer pause I might do some yoga. But that's something that's going to take me half an hour to forty-five minutes to do my routine. But a cigarette is a quick pause ... like a micro-pause.

Ironically, given the well-established association with respiratory maladies, several interviewees reported that smoking breaks provided an opportunity to calm themselves down by regulating their breathing. Asked to explain the attraction of smoking a cigarette during these breaks rather than just leaving the office getting some fresh air, Leroy said:

> Probably just taking a deep breath. Even though it's not fresh air. But having that deep inhale. It just relaxes you because you're taking a deeper breath than you would usually.

This was not an exceptional observation:

> It gives me a stimulus, the stimulus being the inhalation. I mean, it's forcing you to breathe. It's slowing your breathing down and making you more relaxed. (Karen)

> It's a regulation of your breathing, isn't it, because you're slowing yourself down ... your breathing's slowing down ... so everything's not pushing forward at a hundred miles an hour. The meditation factor is big. (Willie)

In this sense, pauses serve as a relief from suffocation. Coming up for air (Orwell, 1939/2021).

Thirdly, interviewees described how they used smoking breaks to literally witness the world around them; to connect in some physical sense with the city that they might otherwise only behold through an office window. Magda, a care worker in a residential home, who goes outside several times a day to vape, explained that:

> I like to go outside and sit on the bench and watch people. I like to watch how they behave, how they just go around like headless chickens. I like to observe how people react to certain situations and how they go through their days ... and I think about what I would do in this situation. I'm learning from their mistakes ... or learning from them if they do something smart.

Karen regularly walks from the hospital building where she works to a nearby graveyard:

> Sometimes me and my colleague walk round there and don't say anything because ... because you do absorb what you're walking through.

Patty, who was working from home during the pandemic, found herself discovering her local area during her brief smoking pauses:

> I might just have a glance at the street or notice a bird overhead. I'll notice the weather; if there's any kind of things going on in the back street; if there's anybody outside their houses I'll probably watch them.

Harry's office is in the city centre and he finds coming out from its stuffiness to the urban bustle quite exhilarating:

It's a really busy area: fire engines, police cars flying by ... it's so windy down there that a few people get blown over. It's quite entertaining, to be completely honest.

He tells a story about how he was standing outside his office building watching the world go by a few weeks ago and a famous boxer walked past. Harry struck up a conversation with him. They spoke for just a few minutes, but it made Harry's day. There is luxury hotel near his office block and now he finds himself looking out for other celebrities who might be entering or leaving it.

When speaking about witnessing the city, our interviewees saw smoking breaks as a mode of urban re-entry. They saw their workplaces as somehow cut off from the city; within it but disconnected from its vibrant energy. They regarded work pauses as occasions for reorientation, allowing them to relate the intramural routines of work to a broader social context.

A fourth function of smoking breaks is as time markers, often pointing to transitions within the structure of the working day. Work time is clock-time. Workers focus upon where they are in the habitual process of the day that they have sold to their employer. As Patty puts it:

I like to have a cigarette when I start work for the day and then I finish ... So, there are always like these habitual markers in the day. I always have a cigarette at this point and that allows for the transition into the next part of the day.

Harry told us that:

I've never been one to have a massive urge to smoke. I think it's more when I'm in a routine of smoking at work, I'll stick to that routine. It's not like I'm sitting there gagging because I need a smoke. It's more periodically at the times when I would normally go for a smoke, I'm looking at the clock thinking in my head, 'I'm gonna go for a smoke in ten minutes'.

But there is more than marking time going on here. Interviewees told us about their efforts to recapture some of their own time. The break becomes a moment of tactical reparation. Harry explained that he saw smoking breaks as an opportunity to take back some of his time from the bosses:

To be honest, I can take the piss a bit with it. If you know it's a Friday and you're thinking 'OK, I've got three hours left to go. If I can get two or three cig breaks in there that will knock half an hour off my day.

Leroy was equally candid:

It's like, I've absorbed X amount of bullshit. I get a bit of payback if you will.

Karen explains that smoking breaks allow staff members to complain about their bosses. Asked why she needs to be outside to do this, she says:

Because there's nobody else listening to your whinges and gripes. You're free.

As interviewees described their experiences of work pauses it soon became clear that these were far from moments of existential emptiness in which they 'did nothing'. On the contrary, pauses were spoken of as occasions for getting things done with a view to making the working day more bearable, tractable and perhaps survivable. They are periods of 'awayness' from submission to the rhythms of unfree labour in which people flee from alienating demands while preparing themselves for a return to these temporarily erased burdens.

Although described as smoking breaks, the acts of smoking or vaping as such seemed marginal to the experiences that our interviewees described to us. According to their accounts, they were not simply pausing to smoke, but smoking as part of a ritual of pausing. If the cigarette provided the ostensible reason for leaving the workplace, it was the sensation of being away that made these breaks so compelling.

We became convinced of the need to look beyond the smoke at what was really going on. Historically, the industrial city has tended to be imagined through a haze of smoke which, while defining its ambience, can serve to blur important relational details. The smoke, after all, is merely a vaporous effect of social forces that can be much more suffocating in their intangibility than the polluted atmosphere itself. We could certainly look at smokers as we saw them scattered across the city as victims of senseless habit. (Neither of us smoke, and the temptation to judge had to be resisted.) But we were more interested in making sense of this repetitious ritual as a response to the city. In what ways were these people sustaining, interrupting, escaping from or blending into an urban rhythm? How could these inconspicuous pauses in which reflection, breathing, observing and time-marking occurred be visually witnessed? How did people know how to 'do pausing', as the ethnomethodologists might put it? To answer these questions, we had to move from the listening posture of the interviewer and walk around the city in the hope of capturing moments in which these transient ritual choreographies were performed.

3. WATCHING SMOKERS

The photographs reproduced in this chapter were taken between 2014 and 2020 within a quarter mile radius of the Leeds City Square, an area that includes the largest number of banking and insurance companies outside of London. The rectangular bold outline applied to the Google Maps view of central Leeds indicates the specific area in which the iterative photographic practice was conducted during the research period (Fig. 1).

This architecturally eclectic area reveals the celebrated Victorian heritage of a post-industrial northern city, with its ubiquitous examples of postmodern 'city living' and regeneration developments, constituting an expedient architectural style familiar to most citizens living in the United Kingdom and continental Europe. Not surprisingly, due to its close proximity to the central railway hub, this affluent 'white-collar' zone is subjected to a steady flow of urban commuters. This large flow of workers attracts a range of 'pilot fish' small businesses to service their needs, including cafes, bars, restaurants, boutique hotels, serviced apartments and the new relocation development for the Channel 4 Television headquarters.

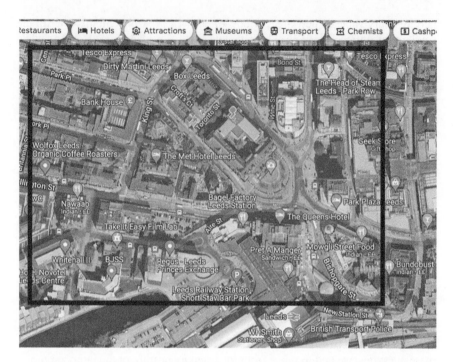

Fig. 1.   Smokers' Research Zone Central Leeds, Google Maps, 2022.

We saw office workers displaying their dangling identity lanyards as if they were medals (Fig. 2). Their break time is about to expire as they snatch one much-needed final inhalation. Time outside the office is precious and the look on their faces is rapt. The city around them seems to have disappeared. They have entered an inner space of reverie. Is it mere coincidence that the lanyard is reversed to anonymise the wearer in the public sphere? Only the magnetic strip of the lanyard is now visible.

Although it is not visible in this version of the photograph, the man in *Smoker wearing a lanyard* (2018) is standing outside a security gate alone. Perhaps this separation from colleagues is important, and smoking provides an excuse for reflective withdrawal. The gate itself carries the warning sign 'private', rendered in large white sans serif characters. Might the presence of this solid impenetrable structure behind the smoker's back suggest a degree of security during an act of vulnerable solitariness?

This photograph explores the precarious liminality that exists between the private performance of smoking and that other performance called work. The implicit message is that office work is so stressful that connection with the cerebral 'inner-world' can only be established away from it.

The revolving door to the office entrance appears calm. The demeanour of the man standing outside it suggests that this activity is part of a regular routine (Fig. 3).

Fig. 2.   Smoker Wearing a Lanyard, 2018. *Source:* Photo by Jim Brogden.

We assume that he is part of the internal security team looking after this prestigious office development. From previous research visits to this site, he appeared to function as a smokers' 'anchor' around which other colleagues feel safe to congregate. He appears to be carefully watching the flow of pedestrians and traffic along Northern Street. What is he thinking about them? How does he imagine his relationship to them across this distance?

The photograph adopts a cinematic viewpoint, framing through the subtle distortions afforded by the expensive beveled glazed exterior. The enlarged left hand accentuates the practised precision of this experienced smoker. Although not evidenced in this photograph, the revolving doors perform their own intake of breath and exhalation as people enter and exit the building. Perhaps we have stumbled here upon the lungs of the city.

The young man taking a mobile phone call whilst smoking is joined by a middle-aged female colleague leaning for support on the emergency exit to their building facing the busy Leeds City Square (Fig. 4). The woman concentrates on breathing before the next pull on the cigarette. The cigarette seems to function as a breathing prosthetic, a metronome of breath. The photograph highlights the haptic performance required through the literal indexing of the woman's red painted fingernails gripping the foreshortened cigarette. The photograph's narrative function suggests that these two smokers are colleagues, not strangers.

Fig. 3. Smoker Outside Office Reception, 2017. *Source:* Photo by Jim Brogden.

Fig. 4. Two Smokers Facing City Square, 2019. *Source:* Photo by Jim Brogden.

There is an atavistic tendency suggested by their occupancy of this external space transformed into a cave, which serves to reinforce their connectedness to their workplace, whilst offering some control over external air circulation, traffic noise and pedestrian flow. The photograph allows the viewer to reflect on the explicit sharing of air in an enclosed but open space, where the solitariness of smoking has now been replaced by a collaborative performance between two colleagues.

The two smokers located off Albion Street have chosen a more exposed position (Fig. 5). Protected from behind by the brown brick façade they enact a prescient 'social distancing'. The photograph captures the man and woman at the moment that each exhales and inhales; an all-consuming hedonistic performance that offers a masterclass in how to smoke in public without disrupting the movement of fellow citizens. They have both 'hit their mark' in a theatrical sense, totally absorbed and oblivious to any ensuing claims on their time. Their apparent satisfaction and equanimity create a mood that showcases the meditative benefits of open-air pauses to breathe freely (Fig. 6).

It appears that smokers in the city choose specific locations for their ritual enactments. One consideration in choosing a place to smoke might include where best to observe the city's transient narratives. Were the smokers we observed involved in their own inadvertent ethnographic observations, in which their act of smoking functioned as a convenient decoy? Smokers observe in an almost hypnagogic state between their interior and exterior lives. Tracking and scanning the movement of traffic, pedestrians and voyeuristic researchers, they engage in the pleasure of observation for its own sake.

Fig. 5. Two Smokers off Albion Street, Leeds, 2014. *Source:* Photo by Jim Brogden.

Fig. 6.   Feel Good, 2014. *Source:* Photo by Jim Brogden.

Exposed in strong light from the right of frame, the young man in the grey suit in *Feel Good* (2014) checks his mobile phone whilst observing the photographer pointing the digital camera at him. The multi-tasking on display is impressive, but not uncommon. The 'Feel Good' slogan across his Boots' branded bag provides an ironic referent when we notice the relaxed grip of the right hand holding the cigarette. We might infer from this duel of gazes between photographer and subject that it could easily be reinterpreted as subject encountering subject. The confident posture of the young man dressed in a smart business suit suggests he is used to being observed. We infer perhaps from his enquiring gaze that he understands why the photographer has chosen him. One further explanation for his apparent ease at being photographed is the notion that comfort with being photographed is generationally related. For digital natives there is nothing new in such observation of their activity as observers.

Many photographs feature smoking as an accessory to mobile phone use. And in some sense the two activities (addictions? pleasures?) could be seen to alternate, to relieve or preclude feelings of anxiety. In this context, the photograph shows that the intervals between inhaling the smoke and exhaling the smoke cannot be wasted, as there are messages to check and people to connect with.

We noticed how some office workers stood well away from their places of employment, as if seeking to escape from even the shadow of unfree labour, even

Fig. 7.   Smoker Standing Outside Mill Hill Chapel, 2018. *Source:* Photo by
Jim Brogden.

if that means being stranded in the no-man's land of public space. The man standing outside Mill Hill Chapel looks pensively towards the city, the gates behind him form shadows on the pavement somehow symbolising an escape plan (Fig. 7).

There are moments when smokers appear to be in between significant moments. The two men smoking on Russell Street embody an anxiety, maybe reacting to something that has just happened; perhaps anticipating a brewing problem (Fig. 8). Might they be co-workers who can only speak freely away from the ears of the office? Their shared act of smoking seems to serve as a conversational lubricant; an occasion to pause within the pause. Of course, we can only speculate on the conversation represented in this photograph, but the choice of location is interesting, as it is away from any obvious office main entrance. There are no windows nearby from which their conversation might be overheard. The particular framing of this photograph perpetuates the paranoid mood. Covert architectural space is appropriated from across Russell Street to achieve a mood of surveillance. As a consequence, the photograph's visual syntax encourages the spectator to hypothesise on the nature of this urban drama situated in the extreme right third of the photograph.

The parallels between mobile phone use and smoking are obvious. In each activity there is the same haptic absorption, providing a reason to be still. They legitimise apparent inactivity, for the individual user is still doing something. Is this a paradoxical alibi for stillness, conflating the commodification of the present moment with the desire to take back lost time from the workplace?

Fig. 8.   Two Smokers in Conversation on Russell Street, 2016. *Source:* Photo by Jim Brogden.

Fig. 9.   Smoker in Telephone Box, 2020. *Source:* Photo by Jim Brogden.

The photograph of the young man 'multi-tasking' in the telephone box seems bizarre (Fig. 9). Why would someone enter a now anachronistic telephone box to use a mobile phone? One possible reading suggests that the man needed a quiet place in the shade to check his mobile messages, away from the glare of direct daylight. And ironically, an available space is provided by a redundant telephone box. The photograph shows the door to the telephone box is open, or missing, which allows the man's cigarette smoke to drift into the open air. The exhaled plume of smoke is suspended above the text message, thereby accentuating the absorptive mood. The preoccupations of both the young male smoker on the right of this diptych and female smoker through the telephone box structure on the left allow the photographer to create a frontal cinematic aesthetic. The photographer delights in the perceptual challenges offered by these structures and surfaces. The camera's own shutter as breath inhales the visual subject – capturing the transient iterations of everyday smoking in the city.

4. NO SMOKE WITHOUT BURN OUT

The city is a space in which people are called upon to employ both attention and inattention; the former to its routes, rhythms and routines; the latter to the presence of strangers with whom the space must be shared, but whose existence cannot be fully registered. In an excellent study of urban indifference, Fran Tonkiss (2003, p. 300) observes that:

> What appears as dissociation is, in fact, the basic form of urban sociation, one that allows us to coexist with all these largely unknown others. Not interacting with others in this sense becomes a primary condition for urban social life, securing individual calm together with relative social peace.

It is through this tension between being thrown together and pulling away that people come to experience the city and make meaning of it. It is in moments of pause that this tension comes closer to the surface of consciousness, regulating the beat of attention and inattention by taking the performative pressure off of each. This release is not a luxury, but a necessity. Without such distractions urban dwellers are driven to another kind of distraction.

In offering more than the senses can digest at any one time, the city, however bright its lights, rich its pickings or exciting its speed, induces regular burps of overload which are not impolite accidents, but inevitable effects of a congested sensorium. The urban impulse to pause intermittently in order to resume the performance of sociality reflects a need to reduce the intensity of focused involvement. In *Behavior in Public Places*, Erving Goffman (1963, p. 43) discusses a distinction between main and side involvements:

> A main involvement is one that absorbs the major part of an individual's attention and interest, visibly forming the principal current determinant of his actions. A side involvement is an activity that an individual can carry on in an abstracted fashion without threatening of confusing simultaneous maintenance of a main involvement.

Goffman goes on to suggest why people are attracted to subordinate involvements, using terms that reflect our own findings:

> Given the fact that a subordinate involvement provides a diversion of self from a dominant involvement, even if this diversion is felt to be of a minor kind, we may expect that when a dominant involvement seems to threaten the security of an individual and his self-control within the situation, he may initiate or affect a subordinate involvement in order to show that he is in command of his circumstances. (1963, p. 49)

Smoking breaks serve as moments of breakaway from the dominating involvement of the commercial city. It is a minor act of resistance against the situational obligations of urban life. We are reminded here of Brigitte Stegers' (2004) intriguing account of how Japanese workers, the most sleep-deprived in the world, have acquired the habit of taking short naps in the course of their working day. Known as *inemuri*, the term describes being asleep while still being present, in contrast to night-time sleeping which is separate from the involvement obligations of the workplace. The polychronic nature of cities, whereby experiences and commitments do not happen consecutively but simultaneously, turns involvement and respite into acts that must appear to happen synchronously. Within the regime of urban rhythm, being present and being absent must be performed at the same time.

Need this be so? We might conclude that smoking in the street or napping in the office are hardly the most efficacious ways of seeking relief. As Majda, the care-home worker, told us when we asked her what a visitor from another planet would make of people standing outside their places of work smoking and vaping:

> These are humans. Humans are stupid. We like to suck on things that we think make us free, but are basically killing us. But we like them because they make us feel like they're helping us.

Goffman's empirical account of 'away' activities describes well the strategies that urban workers adopt in the face of usurping involvements, but does not touch on the normative question of whether such grab-and-run retreats are the best way of living well in cities. Some urban scholars have begun to consider the value of creating 'quiet spaces' within cities (Booi & Van den Berg, 2012; Nielsen, Jørgensen, & Braae, 2016; Quercia, Schifanella, & Aiello, 2014). While surely valuable, such institutionalised spaces of retreat conform to an urban order within which tranquillity is an exotic exception to the tyranny of polychronic culture. The question for us is whether there might be more to urban deceleration than pausing. Might the urban pause be stretched to a point that it challenges the compulsion of the city's rhythmic order?

For this to happen, we would need to move beyond essentialist notions of the city as a space dominated by forms of economic involvement which reduce everything else to subordinate, marginal or insignificant involvements. The research on which this chapter is based was conducted with a view to exploring how one such seemingly empty act of passing time reflects urban aspirations that are broader and deeper than are visible at first sight. Watching and hearing about the experiential texture of urban pauses as moments of reflection, meditative breathing, surveillance and time marking raises questions about how else urban cultures could make room for these vital human activities.

REFERENCES

Booi, H., & Van den Berg, F. (2012). Quiet areas and the need for quietness in Amsterdam. *International Journal of Environmental Research and Public Health, 9*(4), 1030–1050.

Crompton, J. L. (2013). The health rationale for urban parks in the nineteenth century in the USA. *World Leisure Journal, 55*(4), 333–346.

Eiser, J. R., Sutton, S. R., & Wober, M. (1977). Smokers, non-smokers and the attribution of addiction. *British Journal of Social & Clinical Psychology, 16*(4), 329–336.

Fedele, M., & Borland, R. (1998). Characteristics of exiled smoking from workplaces. *Psychology and Health, 13*(3), 545–554.

Fitzgerald, D., Rose, N., & Singh, I. (2016). Living well in the Neuropolis. *The Sociological Review, 64*(1_suppl), 221–237.

Gandy, M. (2020). Urban atmospheres. In *Being urban* (pp. 89–112). Abingdon, Oxon: Routledge.

Goffman, E. (1961). *Asylums: Essays on the social situation of mental patients and other inmates.* Piscataway, NJ: Aldine Transaction.

Goffman, E. (1963). *Behavior in public places.* New York, NY: Free Press.

Gubrium, J. F., & Holstein, J. A. (2002). From the individual interview to the interview society. In *Handbook of interview research: Context and method* (pp. 3–32). Newcastle upon Tyne: Sage.

Milgram, S. (1970). The experience of living in cities. *Science, 167*(3924), 1461–1468.

Navaro-Yashin, Y. (2009). Affective spaces, melancholic objects: Ruination and the production of anthropological knowledge. *The Journal of the Royal Anthropological Institute, 15*(1), 1–18.

Nielsen, H. W., Jørgensen, G., & Braae, E. (2016). Big cities –'Quiet places': Tracing relationships between material and immaterial qualities of urban spaces. *SPOOL, 3*(1), 67–82.

Orwell, G. (1939/2021). *Coming up for air.* Oxford: Oxford University Press.

Pykett, J., Osborne, T., & Resch, B. (2020). From urban stress to neurourbanism: How should we research city well-being? *Annals of the Association of American Geographers, 110*(6), 1936–1951.

Quercia, D., Schifanella, R., & Aiello, L. M. (2014, September). The shortest path to happiness: Recommending beautiful, quiet, and happy routes in the city. In *Proceedings of the 25th ACM conference on Hypertext and social media* (pp. 116–125).

Simmel, G. (1964). *The web of group-affiliations.* New York, NY: Free Press.

Snow, R. P., & Brissett, D. (1986). Pauses: Explorations in social rhythm. *Symbolic Interaction, 9*(1), 1–18.

Steger, B. (2004). *Negotiating sleep patterns in Japan.* Abingdon, Oxon: Routledge.

Tonkiss, F. (2003). The ethics of indifference: Community and solitude in the city. *International Journal of Cultural Studies, 6*(3), 297–311.

Trentmann, F., & Normal, D. I. (2009/2020). Blackouts, breakdowns and the elasticity of everyday life. In *Time, consumption and everyday life: Practice, materiality and culture.* Oxford: Oxford University Press.

Trougakos, J. P., & Hideg, I. (2009). Momentary work recovery: The role of within-day work breaks. In *Current perspectives on job-stress recovery.* Bingley: Emerald Publishing Limited.

Turner, V. (1974). Liminal to liminoid, in play, flow, and ritual: An essay in comparative symbology. *Rice Institute Pamphlet-Rice University Studies, 60*(3), 53–92.

Chapter 5

WHAT WE SEE (AND WHAT WE DON'T): RESIGNIFYING URBAN TRACES OF COLONIALISM

Giovanni Semi and Annalisa Frisina

ABSTRACT

The purpose of this chapter is twofold: in the first part, we will provide compre-hensive, state-of-the-art urban and visual studies across the domains of visibility, urban aesthetics and the legitimate use of the urban. We will show that what we see is foremost what is accessible and legitimate as a vision, while the urban provides multiple realms of invisibility that are often neglected or rendered invisible. Art, architecture, urbanism and place-making will be used as examples of these dynamics.

In the second part of the chapter, we will present a research study on the decolonial practices of re-signification of colonial urban traces. Despite the dominant representation of Italians as 'good people' (a local version of 'white innocence'), in recent years, Italy has witnessed a new interest stemming from bottom-up local movements dealing with colonial legacy in the urban space. We will show a research example ('Decolonising the City. Visual Dialogues in Padova') based on participatory video, arts-based methods and walking methods.

Keywords: (In)visibility regime; urbanism; participatory visual research; decolonial sociology; urban regeneration; multiculturalism

1. INTRODUCTION

The urban realm has always struck the imagination of the newcomer, the trav-eller, the foreigner, by reason of what it reveals, the ability to stimulate the imagination, to amaze a trained gaze to other visions and stimuli. We might even

Visual and Multimodal Urban Sociology, Part B
Research in Urban Sociology, Volume 18B, 125–142
Copyright © 2023 by Emerald Publishing Limited
ISSN: 1047-0042/doi:10.1108/S1047-00422023000018B005

consider that one of the reasons for global urbanisation is precisely related to a visual pull factor, an attractive capacity that cities have elevated to a political project.

Over the centuries, and especially in the twentieth century, the arts have contributed particularly to the cultural industry and cinema with their ability to depict and translate, represent and circulate representations. Cinematic cities are born precisely for that: places such as New York and Paris become visually known without people even having experienced them.

Both what we recognise as a visual trace and what is shown to us as desirable, pleasant and beautiful make up the visible, a kingdom constantly equipped to produce regimes of visibility (Brighenti, 2007; De Backer, 2019; Gilman, 1995), that is, social legitimations to recognise traces with respect to others, signs over other signs, forms of knowledge over other forms of knowledge.

The public space redeveloped by signature architecture, urban design and greening interventions is visible, such as the New York High Line (Loughran, 2016; Semi & Bolzoni, 2020), and a commercial streetscape is visible, with coloured signs and cosmopolitan references (Zukin, 2012).

However, not everything that exists is visible, that is, socially legitimised for visual recognition. From what is considered ugly and hidden, to what is not visited and therefore left out of the tourist circuits (and disappears from visual social networks, such as Instagram or Facebook), to what must not be seen because it is disorienting or destabilising, such as an informal urban settlement or a place of detention, there is a whole world that lives within a regime of invisibility (Topak, 2019).

Following the recent literature on what Böhme calls 'aesthetic capitalism' (2017), taking up Sloterdijk's insights into immunisations and bubbles (2011) and integrating Edensor's reading on light and dark (2017), we intend to offer here a theoretical frame on the urban as a machine for legitimising visibility and invisibility.

2. VISIBILITY REGIMES THROUGH TIME

Following Therborn (2017), we can see cities as those contexts where the concentration of wealth and power is maximum, while the urban is a widespread, global network that connects cities in a material and immaterial network of infrastructures, flows and mobilities (Brenner & Schmid, 2015). Historically, the making of urban centres, of cities, happened through the capacity to concentrate wealth and power under the affirmation of each specific economic system. With regards to our era, capitalism and its continuous mutations and variegations define urban form. We can, somewhat hastily, distinguish at least three different periods of urban development over the last 150 years that are characterised by equally different visibility regimes: Fordist urbanism, post-Fordist urbanism and platform urbanism.

By Fordist urbanism, we mean the specific urbanisation based upon industrial manufacturing development. The factory spread everywhere on a global level as the main cornerstone of this urbanism, together with the rigid functional separation between residential neighbourhoods and workplaces. If the affirmation of this model follows the temporalities of each national capitalism and adapts to pre-existing urban forms (where they existed), for example by creating industrial cities along the lines of the Renaissance or medieval cities in Europe, or brand new settlements becoming rapidly industrial cities in North America or parts of Asia, however, this model began to collapse when global competition and energy crises drew new maps of power after World War II. It is no coincidence that so-called 'shrinking cities' spread earlier and with particular violence in the Western part of the Global North as early as the late 1950s. This Fordist urbanism has its own regime of visibility and legitimacy, inherent in the modern metropolis, as Simmel keenly noted when looking at fin-de-siècle Berlin (1902). It is linked to the domination of the eye as a 'social' sense, of its preponderance with respect to the 'ear'. The metropolis can be seen. This characteristic of understanding the world we inhabit has a material, structural and even industrial dimension. The factory shows itself, in its majesty, to have its own representations. As in the murals of Diego Rivera, it becomes a recognisable element in its materiality and in the serial reproduction of its architecture, with the chimney, the red brick and the majestic occupation of land.

Illegitimate and therefore often invisible to the eye was everything that escaped the rigid temporality and spatiality of Fordist urbanism: from the refusal of work to the different segregations that also characterised this urbanism, such as gender segregation within the nuclear and patriarchal family or the racial one. When applying the lens of intersectionality, invisibility regimes become even more compelling, as in the case of the white industrial worker as opposed to Black female workers (Jordan-Zachery, 2013).

When de-industrialisation took over, the uneven dissolution of Fordist urbanism left cities filled with 'urban voids', sometimes similar to craters, in other cases hidden by the facades of the previous city and some small improvements. The urban landscape was deprived of its previous function, use and legitimate imagery. Factories emptied, dismantled and reassembled in other areas of the world, workers' neighbourhoods devoid of life and devastated by the spread of mass unemployment and heroin, urban rhythms shaken by the 'conquest of the night' (Melbin, 1978), subcultures rapidly becoming youth cultures, made the industrial city almost unrecognisable.

Post-Fordist urbanism slowly and progressively filled those gaps with new functions, from the tertiary city to the myriad variegated gentrifications (Smith, 2005), passing through the plastic capacity of capitalism to take possession of ruins and their aesthetics as well, as the literature on ruin porn has masterfully shown (Edensor, 2005; Lyons, 2018).[1] Cities went from managerial to entrepreneurial status, as David Harvey (1989) shows, and started strategies of reciprocal competition through cultural, sport and commercial events (Smith, 2012). The visibility regime of the post-Fordist city plays on the double register of the

---

[1]The concept of 'ruin porn' applies to the ambiguous relationship with the visual appropriation of ruins, both made of pleasure and guilt.

aestheticization of the industrial past and on the production of festive and pyrotechnic imaginaries, with an emphasis on the production of cosmopolitan and sanitised public spaces, safe and purified from any form of conflict that can even remember the industrial city and its infinite contradictions (Mitchell, 2003). As Terry Clark points out, this was the making of a 'city as entertainment machine' (2003), an urban environment that economically and symbolically enhances various amenities, whether environmental, such as waterfronts, or cultural, such as museums and cafes. What cannot and must not be seen is therefore the past, whether it is colonial or industrial, unless it passes through its own process of aestheticization, and also everything that does not seem to contribute to the consumption of this entertainment machine. For example, numerous forms of neoliberal governmental strategies also spread, such as the business improvement districts, where the state renounces its function of managing and controlling the public space by delegating it to a coalition of private actors (Peyroux, Pütz, & Glasze, 2012). Privatisation is a salient feature of this urbanism, almost as much as the public nature of the Fordist urban was omnipresent (Peck, 2010). It follows that those who do not have the economic means or the social legitimacy to participate in post-Fordist urbanism fill the ranks of the undesirable or dangerous.

At the turn of the new millennium, however, the post-Fordist city also began a phase of further mutation, the result of two intertwined sets of phenomena: on one hand, the repeated economic and financial crises inaugurated by the bursting of the dot-com bubble in the mid-1990s, passing through the sub-prime mortgage crisis of the early 2000s and up to the pandemic crisis that began in 2020, and on the other hand, the technological accelerations that happened in the same period to enhance the affirmation of digital companies and multiple platforms. In the new millennium began what seems to be an urbanisation of platforms, where the geography of servers, global logistics of goods and services and the interpenetration between devices and the experience of the world becomes more and more intense and digitalised (Hodson, Kasmire, McMeekin, Stehlin, & Ward, 2020).

The visibility regime that begins to emerge, although we are only at the beginning of this transformation, passes through a new domination by the eye, albeit digitally. The renderings, the growing multiplication of visual social networks such as Instagram or TikTok, increasingly mediate our experience of reality and the urban by superimposing visual layers on top of other visual layers, accelerating the present on other temporal dimensions. If the analogic urban form remains the one in which the corporeal dimension of human experience finds its place, digital acceleration pushes many of these bodies to equally accelerated uses of space. We can see two phenomena, antithetical to each other, as representative of this urbanism: global tourism and home working.

Certainly, global tourism has strongly expanded, democratised and universalised during post-Fordist urbanism, both for geopolitical reasons, such as the expansion of globalisation to tourist markets previously excluded to mass audiences, and for reasons of diffusion of well-being and styles of consumerist life that were previously closed to the vast majority of the world (Urry & Larsen, 2011). If, in the Fordist era, only the rich and highly skilled workers also travelled for tourism (think of the birth, in those times, of global congresses and fairs), starting in the 1970s and 1980s, we saw a first global expansion of tourism, as evidenced also by the geography of air hubs and the incredible acceleration of intercontinental flights. As the works of Arjun Appadurai (1996) and John Urry (2012) have shown so powerfully, tourism globalisation was also a globalisation of visual imaginaries and mutual gazes. However, with the birth of logistics and rental platforms, such as Airbnb or Booking.com, global tourism will mark a decisive break with the past, redefining the old tourism industry (hotels) and making the urban a potential value extraction site (Cocola-Gant, Gago, & Jover, 2020; Semi & Tonetta, 2021). The standardisation of the visual imaginaries of global tourism has been a formidable vector for the expansion of the sector, like IKEA's interior furnishings and a few other global designers and manufacturers. This use of space, however, is characterised by being short term, accelerated and temporary, Fordist in rhythms and post-Fordist in uses.

The same platforms that allow us, or allowed us before the pandemic, to move so quickly on a global level, are also those, by taking advantage of the pandemic, that have helped us segregate ourselves inside our homes, making the dialectic between inside and outside, so peculiar for the urban rhythms, extreme and in favour of the interior. Infinite forms of housing segregation, imposed by states and companies but also chosen by many workers who have thus stopped living as commuters, are redesigning the urban form in unexpected and unpredictable ways (Zukin, 2020). Think of the office workspace, the subject of powerful visual representations, from cinema to TV series (a compendium of the cultural history of the office is masterfully obtained from the TV series *Mad Men* and *The Office*): what real and visual future does this space have given the discovery that home working increases productivity and decreases costs?

In terms of visibility and invisibility, legitimacy and illegitimacy, the urbanisation of platforms is still to be discovered, but several traces are already emerging. Social and urban inequalities are grafted onto digital acceleration, as shown by the social types of riders and freight logistics drivers, subject to forms of urban exploitation more similar to those of the late nineteenth century than of the late twentieth century. The dynamics of home working also lead to new and unexpected regimes of invisibility, where domestic violence and radical housing inequalities flourish both in terms of housing affordability and in terms of psychological well-being.

3. THE DIALECTICS BETWEEN VISIBILITY AND INVISIBILITY

This brief historical-sociological excursus between urban form, regimes of economic accumulation and consequent visibility and invisibility now leads us to think in more abstract terms on what we have up to now defined as regimes of visibility (Brighenti, 2007).

As Sharon Zukin wrote, 'culture is what cities do best' (1996), referring to the development of one of the engines of contemporary capitalism, which she called the symbolic economy. In her words, this economy is based on two parallel production systems: 'the production of space, with its synergy of capital investment and cultural meanings, and the production of symbols, which constructs both a currency of commercial exchange and a language of social identity' (Zukin, 1996, p. 24). Cities are those sites where the symbolic economy is created and spread and become all the more important when what Böhme calls 'aesthetic capitalism' is grafted, where space takes on value as a staging of reality (2017). To take up reflections of an aesthetic nature, as in the case of Ranciére's (2021) emancipated spectator, the spectacularising of the representative dimension of reality across the centuries becomes more and more public, widespread and even subject to collective criticism. However, it also enters the commercial circuit, generating new and continuous value just by being exchanged. The urban becomes part of this spectacle and further exchange.

If we take the example of global tourism, the passage from the eighteenth-century or nineteenth-century Grand Tour by the European élite to the temporary use of accommodations rented on Airbnb in recent years, this tells of a double transformation: the democratisation of the exploitation of space by many inhabitants of the world, but also a growing reliance on images and representations of reality increasingly consumed and disconnected from the mechanisms of production. You buy your own experience on a website well before you visit the actual site.

What, then, are visibility regimes? We consider them as frames. They work as Goffman (1974) showed: they tell you what to see and how to see it, and above all they hide what is outside the frame. Returning to Tim Edensor's studies of cultural geography, we can also think of visibility regimes as 'ways of seeing and interpreting landscapes [that depend] on its material qualities, their interaction with light and our sensory experience, as well as being informed by intersubjective cultural understandings and values' (2017, p. 22).

Seeing and not seeing therefore imply a constant swing between a subjective and intersubjective dimension, between individual agency and the materiality of the social structure.

Culturally, we are used to associating what is seen with light and illumination, relegating the invisible to dimensions devoid of or deprived of light, where darkness takes on a double meaning both as a territory where things that cannot or must not be seen happen but also as a realm that protects precisely those people and things that cannot or must not be seen.

The struggle for visibility is therefore a struggle to get out of the state of invisibility and illegitimacy that also involves a redesign and resignification of what light and darkness should be. It is therefore no coincidence that we have chosen post-colonial practices of struggle as a terrain to show this constant dialectic between the visible and the invisible.

4. WHY RESIGNIFY URBAN TRACES OF COLONIALISM?

Decolonising cities in Europe has become a way to come to terms with a denied history of imperialism, colonialism, racism and enduring structural violence.

As Valeria Deplano (2020) has argued, in most cases it is institutions, particularly state institutions, that choose who or what is worthy of being remembered. In Europe, colonial events, scattered like traces in cities, have helped celebrate national histories steeped in colonialist values. What falters today are not only the statues and street names but also the worldviews and social hierarchies that erected those statues and named those streets. It is white innocence (Wekker, 2016) with its privileges that is being challenged in a post-colonial and post-migratory Europe in which its citizens have been of the most diverse origins for generations and in which the activism of Afro-descendants becomes increasingly relevant.

According to Schilling (2020), the idea of decolonising the cities of Europe has spread and grown in recent years. For example, in Germany, since 2007, Berlin Postkolonial has been working to bring traces of Germany's colonial past out of oblivion in its institutions, monuments and street names. Through its digital activism, urban walks and cultural events, Berlin Postkolonial succeeded in renaming a street that previously honoured the slave trader Otto Friedrich von der Gröben. The street now celebrates and acquaints a wider audience with May Ayim, a German Afro-descendant, scholar-activist, poet and pioneer in the valorisation of the history of Afro-Germans.

In The Netherlands, it is thanks to Afro-descendant activists (primarily Simone Zeefuik, Hodan Warsame and Tirza Balk) that a major decolonisation process was initiated at the Tropenmuseum in Amsterdam (van Huis, 2019). This led not only to a critical revision of how colonialism was (not) being told in the museum, but in 2019 gave rise to a new exhibition entitled 'Afterlives of Slavery', within which, for example, video interviews with scholars such as Gloria Wekker were projected on large screens to make people rethink the close relations between the colonial past, contemporary social inequalities and anti-racist struggles in Dutch and European society.

Anti-racist movements thus seem increasingly engaged in practices of cultural re-signification at the urban level. The statues, monuments, museums and streets steeped in colonial history often remain but are flanked by plaques or cultural and political interventions that bring them out of invisibility. This prevents them from being seen in an innocent, uncritical way. Sometimes, compensatory interventions also take place, erecting new statues and monuments, creating innovative exhibitions and changing street names to celebrate figures of anti-colonial and anti-racist resistance.

The accusation of wanting to 'erase history' seems specious because it is instead a call to know it better in a critical key and to decolonise the gaze on contemporary European society.

In Italy, material traces of colonialism are in almost every city, as can be seen from the (interactive) map 'Viva Zerai!'[2] or the website of the project 'Postcolonial Italy – Mapping Colonial Heritage'.[3] These traces in the past have helped to celebrate a national history steeped in colonialist values of racial superiority and inferiority, only to fall into invisibility and remain long forgotten. Starting with the global mobilisations linked to the Black Lives Matter movement of 2020 (following the murder of George Floyd in the United States), initiatives have multiplied in Italy to bring out of indifference the names of historical figures and places linked to the violent history of Italian colonialism.[4] Streets, squares and monuments provide the chance to start a public debate on a silenced colonial history. As Igiaba Scego, an Italian writer of Somali origins, clearly states, there is indeed a deep lack of knowledge on colonial history:

> No one tells Italian girls and boys about the squad massacres in Addis Ababa, the concentration camps in Somalia, the gases used by Mussolini against defenceless populations. There is no mention of Italian apartheid (…), segregation was applied in the cities under Italian control. In Asmara the inhabitants of the village of Beit Mekae, who occupied the highest hill of the city, were chased away to create the fenced field, or the first nucleus of the colonial city, an area off-limits to Eritreans. An area only for whites. How many know about Italian apartheid? (Scego, 2014, p. 105)

This lack of knowledge has political roots. Paolo Favero (2010), moving among historical material and contemporary debates on xenophobia and war, explores the self-representation 'Italiani Brava Gente', an image claiming the intrinsic goodness of the Italian people. This representation has its origins in the first Italian colonial enterprises, and it has also been used for overcoming the horrors of fascism. In contemporary Italy, it is evoked for justifying violent events, functioning as an 'ideological laundry' for reformulating and then setting aside events of national shame. Briefly, 'Italiani Brava Gente' is central to the construction of a modern Italy, a nation-state formed in 1871, whose colonial history played a crucial role in building national memory (Deplano & Pes, 2014; Giuliani, 2019).

Ignorance on colonialism can be considered a 'substantive epistemic practice that differentiates the dominant group' (Alcoff, 2007, p. 47). The concept of 'white ignorance' (Mills, 2007) helps us to interpret the selective exclusion of certain historical facts from collective memory as the result of centuries of white

---

[2]https://umap.openstreetmap.fr/fr/map/viva-zerai_519378#6/41.921/16.390.
[3]https://postcolonialitaly.com/.
[4]The most dramatised controversy in the Italian media concerns the statue of journalist Indro Montanelli in Milan (14 June 2020). The statue was covered in red paint with the words 'racist' and 'rapist' written on its base. Montanelli, considered one of the most influential Italian journalists, took part in the fascist invasion of Ethiopia as a voluntary conscript. During his stay, Montanelli took as his 'wife' – under colonial concubinage (the so-called madamato) – 12-year-old Eritrean child named Destà, whom he had bought from her father and who the journalist himself described as a 'little docile animal'. On several occasions, Montanelli justified his act claiming it was an 'African custom'. For a discussion on this controversy, see Pesarini and Panico (2021).

oppression and racial domination. In fact, memory is deeply embedded in power dynamics. Only certain forms of knowledge and ways of remembering have been deemed valid. In opposition to the epistemic practices of the dominant groups, Mills advances the idea of 'counter-memories' produced by minoritised social groups to challenge hegemonic forms of collective memory.

In her book *Roma Negata. Percorsi Postcoloniali Nella Città* (2014), Igiaba Scego works to visually represent the historical connections between Europe and Africa in creative ways; she worked with photographer Rino Bianchi to portray Afro-descendants in places marked by fascism, such as Cinema Impero, Palazzo della Civiltà Italiana and Dogali's stele in Rome. This work represents a significant starting of a dialogue between visual narrations and stories coming from the margins, questioning the Italian colonial past and giving life to forms of counter-memories. *Roma Negata* was a source of inspiration for the realisation of visual research in Padova.

5. DECOLONISING THE CITY. VISUAL DIALOGUES IN PADOVA

Despite its claims to the contrary, whiteness is not a monolithic form. It is fissured, fractured and fragmented, always trying to form a statue. Let's try to work in these "cracks" of whiteness. (Mirzoeff, 2021)

According to Bhambra, Gebrial, and Nişancıoğlu (2018), decolonising means first and foremost a recognition of coloniality as a key to understanding contemporary society. Moreover, it implies a will to build knowledge in alternative ways and a commitment to open new spaces for dialogues with anti-colonial and antiracist movements. Inspired by Walter Mignolo's call for epistemic disobedience and MacDougall's work on transcultural cinema, Albrecht and Walter (2019) argue that it is possible to challenge coloniality with collaborative and self-reflexive filmmaking, which becomes a key method to trigger transcultural processes of understandings.

Following Igiaba Scego (2014), Frisina and a group of graduate students gave life to a visual research project that defied the regime that condemns to invisibility the counter-memories of Italian Afro-descendants. The goal was to explore the historical connections between Europe and Africa in intimate and creative ways, taking urban traces of Italian colonialism in Padova out of insignificance and resignifying them through a participatory video, combined with walking methods and arts-based methods. Participatory and subject-centred approaches (Pauwels & Mannay, 2020, pp. 237–349) allow the treatment of interlocutors as active subjects (not as containers from which to extract useful information), reducing the asymmetric relationship that continues to exist in every observational relationship between a research subject and the researcher. As a university teacher, Frisina wondered what 'decolonizing methods' (Frisina, 2020, pp. 178–186; Smith, 2012; Thambinathan & Kinsella, 2021) could mean in Italy, and with her students she decided to question 'white innocence' and the myth of 'Italiani Brava

Gente' by listening the counter-memories of Italian Afro-descendants and experimenting with practices of counter-visuality (Mirzoeff, 2021), communicating the research to a wider audience and collaborating with local antiracist movements.

The participatory video (Frisina, 2013, pp. 105–113) was the experiential core of the laboratory of the visual research methods course held at the University of Padova in 2020.[5] As Mitchell and de Lange (2020, p. 256) suggest, using participatory video gives participants the opportunity to nurture their reflexivity through a collective work:

> Working with video production as a group process (from the initial concept through the storyboarding, planning shots, shooting, initial screening and post-screening discussion) offers participants access to a type of socially constructed knowledge that is particularly significant to addressing themes which have often been taboo – the unspeakable.

The realisation of the video *Decolonising the City* (Fig. 1) involved a great number of people with different backgrounds, bringing together diverse skills and expertise.[6] The university research laboratory was intertwined with the experience of the collective 'Decolonize your Eyes',[7] born in the Palestro district,[8] where

---

[5]Before the shootings, a day was dedicated to becoming familiar with video cameras and audio recording equipment from the sociology visual laboratory. The shootings spanned a week-and-a-half, during which small groups of students accompanied the Afro-Italian protagonists on their urban walks. The script was partially prepared by the protagonists, and the students negotiated with them the video shootings and the content. After an initial phase of editing, there was a first screening and discussion with the other students, Frisina and people from the collective who helped in the shootings, during which feedbacks and suggestions were gathered. After the first discussion, the videos were shared with the protagonists (one of them, Cadigia, was also a student of the course) and reported feedback. This led to a final editing phase that also required the students to go back to some of the protagonists for extra recordings to be added to the initial narration. This participatory editing lasted for a week-and-a-half, after which followed a final presentation with the class, an official restitution to the protagonists and finally a public restitution in the neighbourhood of Palestro.

[6]Elisabetta Campagni, a master's graduate in Sociology, assisted in the organisation of the course, the shootings and the editing process with the students. Essential assistance came from Dagmawi Yimer, a filmmaker of Ethiopian origin who has been working within the Italian independent cinema industry.

[7]https://www.facebook.com/DecolonizeYourEyes/;   https://resistenzeincirenaica.com/decolonize-your-eyes/; Instagram: Decolonize_Your_Eyes. The symbol chosen by the collective was the Ethiopian partisan Kebedech Seyoum, who upon the death of her husband, killed by Italian colonialists, took command of the anti-colonial guerrilla. The basic aspiration is to connect the anti-fascist resistance in Italy with the anti-colonial one (in tune with the internationalist vision carried out by Resistenze in Cirenaica). https://resistenzeincirenaica.com/tag/federazione-delle-resistenze/.

[8]It is an important neighbourhood also for the memory of the anti-fascist resistance, in which many of its inhabitants participated. The ANPI (National Association of Italian Partisans) from Padua, with its president Floriana Rizzetto, joined Decolonize Your Eyes from the beginning (June 2020).

Fig. 1. Decolonising the City. Visual Dialogues in Padova Link to the Video:
https://www.youtube.com/watch?v=B6CtMsORajE.

most of the colonial traces in Padua are concentrated. In fact, there are many roads that carry colonial names, such as Via Eritrea, Via Asmara, Via Libya, Via Amba Alagi and Via Amba Aradam. They are mostly names of colonial battles and geographic places that were battlegrounds or the locations of war crimes and massacres, though some are the names of Italian war criminals (celebrated as heroes).

The use of walking methods (O'Neill & Roberts, 2020) was motivated by the will to give attention to bodies and their performances, problematising some of the roads and calling out for a different topography. The colonial streets of Padova have been reappropriated by the bodies, voices and gazes of six Italian Afro-descendants[9] who resignified urban traces of colonialism, rereading them though their (family) biographies. We also used arts-based methods (Leavy, 2020) to allow each protagonist of the video to leave a material trace of herself or himself in the public space, a visible sign of her or his counter-memory. The artistic interventions were gifts left in the road or square each participant visited.

Below are reported each protagonist's profile and an insight into her or his personal and political narratives tied to a particular street or square.

Cadigia Hassan was born to an Italian mother and Somali father who was among the first students who reached Italy in the 1960s with a scholarship from the Italian government. She shares the photos of her Italian-Somali family with a friend of hers and then goes to Via Somalia, where she meets a resident living there who has never understood the reason behind the name of that street. This unplanned moment showed how seldom colonial history is known to the larger majority of Italian people and led the students to diverge from the original script. Cadigia has returned to Via Somalia to leave traces of herself, of her family history and of historical intertwining and to make visible the important connections that exist between the two countries.

Ilaria Zorzan is an Italo-Eritrean art history student living in Padova, and she shares her grandparents' story using printed black and white photographs taken by her family members. Her story is narrated while walking among the bridges and canals of Padua. With her family history, Ilaria challenges the colonial propaganda of Italians as 'good people' because they built roads, factories, bridges and other signs of 'civilisation'. Her family biography stands as another side of the history, recalling also the lives of 'mixed children', so-called 'sons of two flags' that included her father. She stresses the hardships they had to go through in the colonies, where interracial marriage was prohibited during fascism. Ilaria conceals her face behind old photographs just to reveal herself in Via Asmara through a mirror.

Cagidia and Ilaria belong to different generations, but both closely deal with their family backgrounds and the history that brought them to Italy. They both work on photographic material in very distinct ways: Cadigia uses photographs belonging especially to her parents, while Ilaria uses photos from her grandparents. The theme of biographical crossroads and historical memory emerges as particularly critical in today's Italian society. Cadigia and Ilaria's contributions bring together a colonial Italian past intertwined with personal memories such as family photographs, which are part of an unknown and more intimate sphere that left scars on thousands of Italian families.

---

[9]The protagonists were involved because they were motivated in various ways to mend stories and interrupted relations between Africa and Italy, and in doing so they placed the colonial fact at the centre in its continuity and contemporaneity.

Artist and activist *Wissal Houbabi* is Italo-Moroccan – 'Mediterranean', as she defines herself. She chose Issaa's song *'Non respiro'* [I can't breathe] (2020) as the soundtrack for her walk through the streets in Padova with colonial names (such as Via Libya, Via Cirenaica), resignifying them through slam poetry.

> We're the children of immigrants who survived the Mediterranean [. . .]. We were looking for a glimmer, to be able to breathe, suffocated even before they shut our mouths and sanitised our hands [. . .]. We're not all in the same boat, and it takes class not to rub it in your face. My social class doesn't have the strength to be angry or bitter.

> [. . .] The past is here, even if you forget it, even if you ignore it, even if you do everything to deny the squalor of what it was, the State that preserves the status of frontiers and jus sanguinis [. . .].

> I'm the reincarnation of the forgotten past [. . .]. I'm Mediterranean, and, here, every story has at least two versions of the truth.

Wissal challenges with her poetry the borders set by racist laws while pasting a map of a capsized Mediterranean region, forcing us to visually subvert dominant points of view. Wissal has spoken publicly as a 'daughter of diaspora and the sea in between', as a 'reincarnation of the removed past'. It is therefore not surprising that not only the direct descendants of the former Italian colonies are taking the floor on these colonial roads, but all those who want to come to terms with the violent history of European capitalist modernity (Danewid, 2021) and who know from direct and daily experience the racism in contemporary society.

Mackda Ghebremariam Tesfau', an Italian-Eritrean scholar and Refugee Welcome activist, reflects upon the neo-colonial international policies between countries that are deeply embedded in the economic capitalist structure of the West. After walking thought the centre of Padova, she reaches the colonial map displayed in Padua's main square that exposes the Italian ex-colonial empire. Her monologue ends by quoting Aimé Césaire's *Discourse on Colonialism* and by leaving his words ('Europe is indefensible') on a reproduction of the colonial map exposed in Piazza delle Erbe (in the historical city centre).

Emmanuel M'bayo Mertens (Fig. 2) is an activist of Arising Africans, an anti-racist association based in Padova. In the video we see him conducting an alternative tour in the historic centre of Padova, in Piazza Antenore, formerly Piazza 9 Maggio. Emmanuel cites the resolution by which the municipality of Padova dedicated the square to the day of the 'proclamation of the empire' proclaimed by Mussolini in 1936. According to Emmanuel, fascism has never completely disappeared, as the Italian citizenship law n. 91/1992 mainly based on *jus sanguinis* shows the racist idea of Italianness being transmitted 'by blood'. Instead, Italy is built upon migration processes, as the story of Antenor, Padova's legendary founder and a refugee, clearly shows. Mertens left a sign reading 'Migration Square' with the colours of the Italian flag. It was a way of re-appropriating negated citizenship, celebrating multiple belongings and performing the on-going transformation of Italianness.

Viviana Zorzato (Figs. 3 and 4) is a painter of Eritrean origin. Her house, full of paintings inspired by Ethiopian iconography, overlooks Via Amba Aradam. In

Fig. 2.   Padova, a City Founded by a Refugee According to Emmanuel
M'bayo Mertens.

everyday language, 'ambaradam' indicates a (generic) confusion. It is a popular
expression in Italy, but few are aware of its origin. Amba Aradam is in fact the
place where in 1936 the Italian colonialists made a massive use of chemical
bombs in violation of the Geneva Convention.

In the video, Viviana tells about her Black women portrait, which she has
repainted numerous times, inspired by *Portrait of a N-word Woman*, a painting
she found years ago and which deeply called her to respond. Doing so meant
taking care of herself, an Afro-descendant Italian woman who has faced sexism
and racism. She tells us to be now at peace with her, and she symbolically opens
her narration by posing one of the portraits she made under the street sign of Via
Amba Aradam. Reflecting on the colonial streets she crosses daily, she argues
that it is important to know the history but also to remember the beauty. Amba
Aradam or Amba Alagi (another street next to her home) cannot be reduced to
colonial violence: they are also names of mountains, and Viviana possesses a free
gaze that sees beauty.

Decolonising the City constitutes a participatory work in which uniqueness is
based on bringing together forms of visual activism from a plurality of actors,
joining academic research and social actions. It asks Italian citizens to come to
terms with the white privilege and innocence that prevents them from seeing the

Figs. 3 and 4. Viviana Zorzato's Gift: Her 'Black Women Portrait', via Amba Aradam.

crimes of colonialism in the urban landscape and structural racism in Italian society.

6. CONCLUDING REMARKS

In this chapter, we have tried to provide a shared perspective on what we see and what we do not see when facing the urban realm. In the first part of this chapter, we set the groundwork for the understanding of visibility regimes. In our understanding, the concept highlights the framing conditions allowing or dis-allowing symbols, icons, traces, signs and real experiences to be seen. We have identified several historical urbanisms, each with a distinct form of visibility. Fordist, post-Fordist and platform urbanisms have transformed the urban realm not only in terms of its fabric but also in terms of what is visible and legitimate and what is beyond that.

In order to explore sociologically what was described in the first part, we offered a grounded understanding of decolonisation as a set of practices that tackle precisely the realm of the visible and the invisible. Through a deep and ethnographic account of the making of an Italian debate on the hidden side of the official colonial history, we presented the results of an ongoing video and participatory tool on the traces of the colonial past. Counter-memories are video-recorded and related to the experiences of the participants in our visual research methods course, combined with walking methods and arts-based methods.

Traces are thus put into scrutiny, just like memories and what can be considered the visible side of history. White privilege arises and is therefore tackled, allowing for a more nuanced understanding of the city as a contested and ongoing text.

REFERENCES

Albrecht, J., & Walter, F. (2019). Judith Albrecht and Florian Walter, epistemic disobedience. Introduction. *Anthrovision*, *7*(2). Retrieved from http://journals.openedition.org/anthrovision/6117. doi:10.4000/anthrovision.6117

Alcoff, L. M. (2007). Epistemologies of ignorance: Three types. In S. Sullivan & N. Tuana (Eds.), *Race and epistemologies of ignorance* (pp. 11–38). Albany, NY: SUNY Press.

Appadurai, A. (1996). *Modernity at large: Cultural dimensions of globalization* (Vol. 1). Minneapolis, MN: University of Minnesota Press.

Bhambra, G., Nişancıoğlu, K., & Gebrial, D. (2018). *Decolonising the university*. London: Pluto Press.

Böhme, G. (2017). *Critique of aesthetic capitalism*. Roma: Mimesis.

Brenner, N., & Schmid, C. (2015). Towards a new epistemology of the urban? *City*, *19*(2–3), 151–182.

Brighenti, A. (2007). Visibility: A category for the social sciences. *Current Sociology*, *55*(3), 323–342.

Clark, T. N. (2003). Urban amenities: Lakes, opera, and juice bars: Do they drive development? In *The city as an entertainment machine*. Bingley: Emerald Publishing Limited.

Cocola-Gant, A., Gago, A., & Jover, J. (2020). Tourism, gentrification and neighbourhood change: An analytical framework–reflections from southern European Cities. In *The overtourism debate*. Bingley: Emerald Publishing Limited.

Danewid, I. (2021). These walls must fall: The black mediterranean and the politics of abolition. In G. Proglio, C. Hawthorne, I. Danewid, P. K. Saucier, G. Grimaldi, A. Pesarini ... V. Gerrand (Eds.), *The black mediterranean. Bodies, borders and citizenship*. London: Palgrave Macmillan.

De Backer, M. (2019). Regimes of visibility: Hanging out in Brussels' public spaces. *Space and Culture*, *22*(3), 308–320.

Deplano, V. (2020). A proposito delle statue e dell'urgenza di decolonizzare l'Europa, in «Storie in movimento». Retrieved from http://storieinmovimento.org/2020/06/13/doveva-accadere/

Deplano, V., & Pes, A. (2014). *Quel che resta dell'impero: la cultura coloniale degli italiani*. Roma: Mimesis.

Edensor, T. (2005). The ghosts of industrial ruins: Ordering and disordering memory in excessive space. *Environment and Planning: Society and Space*, *23*(6), 829–849.

Edensor, T. (2017). *From light to dark: Daylight, illumination, and gloom*. Minneapolis, MN: University of Minnesota Press.

Favero, P. (2010). Italians, the "good people": Reflections on national self-representation in contemporary Italian debates on Xenophobia and war. *Outlines-Critical Practice Studies*, (2), 138–153. Retrieved from http://www.outlines.dk

Frisina, A. (2013). *Ricerca visuale e trasformazioni socio-culturali*. Torino: Utet Università.

Frisina, A. (2020). *Razzismi contemporanei. Le prospettive della sociologia*. Roma: Carocci.

Gilman, S. L. (1995). *Picturing health and illness: Images of identity and difference* (p. 107). Baltimore, MD: Johns Hopkins University Press.

Giuliani, G. (2019). *Race, nation and gender in modern Italy: Intersectional representations in visual culture*. London: Palgrave Macmillan.

Goffman, E. (1974). *Frame analysis: An essay on the organization of experience*. Cambridge, MA: Harvard University Press.

Harvey, D. (1989). From managerialism to entrepreneurialism: The transformation in urban governance in late capitalism. *Geografiska Annaler - Series B: Human Geography*, *71*(1), 3–17.

Hodson, M., Kasmire, J., McMeekin, A., Stehlin, J. G., & Ward, K. (Eds.). (2020). *Urban platforms and the future city: Transformations in infrastructure, governance, knowledge and everyday life.* Abingdon: Routledge.

van Huis, I. (2019). Contesting cultural heritage: Decolonizing the Tropenmuseum as an intervention in the Dutch/European memory complex. In T. Lähdesmäki, L. Passerini, S. Kaasik-Krogerus, & I. van Huis (Eds.), *Dissonant heritages and memories in contemporary Europe* (pp. 215–248). London: Palgrave MacMillan.

Jordan-Zachery, J. (2013). Now you see me, now you don't: My political fight against the invisibility/erasure of black women in intersectionality research. *Politics, Groups, and Identities, 1*(1), 101–109.

Leavy, P. (2020). *Method meets art. Arts-Based research practice* (III ed.). New York, NY: Guilford Press.

Loughran, K. (2016). Imbricated spaces: The High Line, urban parks, and the cultural meaning of city and nature. *Sociological Theory, 34*(4), 311–334.

Lyons, S. (Ed.). (2018). *Ruin porn and the obsession with decay.* London: Palgrave Macmillan.

Melbin, M. (1978). Night as frontier. *American Sociological Review*, 3–22.

Mills, C. W. (2007). White ignorance. In S. Sullivan & N. Tuana (Eds.), *Race and epistemologies of ignorance* (pp. 11–38). Albany: SUNY Press.

Mirzoeff, N. (2021). A moment of clarity. *The Journal of Visual Culture. Palestine Portfolio*, 349–352. doi:10.1177/14704129211046141

Mitchell, D. (2003). *The right to the city: Social justice and the fight for public space.* New York, NY: Guilford Press.

Mitchell, C., & de Lange, N. (2020). Community-based participatory video and social action. In L. Pauwels & D. Mannay (Eds.), *The sage handbook of visual research methods* (254–266). Los Angeles, London: Sage.

O'Neill, M., & Roberts, B. (2020). *Walking methods: Research on the move.* London: Routledge.

Pauwels, L., & Mannay, D. (2020). *The Sage handbook of visual research methods.* Los Angeles, London: Sage.

Peck, J. (2010). *Constructions of neoliberal reason.* Oxford: OUP.

Pesarini, A., & Panico, C. (2021). From Colston to Montanelli: Public memory and counter-monuments in the era of black lives matter. *From the European South, 9*, 99–113. Retrieved from https://www.fesjournal.eu

Peyroux, E., Pütz, R., & Glasze, G. (2012). Business improvement districts (BIDs): The internationalization and contextualization of a 'travelling concept'. *European Urban and Regional Studies, 19*(2), 111–120.

Rancière, J. (2021). *The emancipated spectator.* London: Verso Books.

Scego, I. (2014). *Roma negata. Percorsi postcoloniali nella città.* Roma: Ediesse.

Schilling, B. (2020). Afterlives of colonialism in the everyday: Street names and the (un)making of imperial debris. In B. Sèbe & M. G. Stanard (Eds.), *Decolonising Europe? Popular responses to the end of empire* (pp. 113–139). New York, NY: Routledge.

Semi, G., & Bolzoni, M. (2020). Star architecture and the field of urban design. In *About star architecture* (pp. 55–67). Cham: Springer.

Semi, G., & Tonetta, M. (2021). Marginal hosts: Short-term rental suppliers in Turin, Italy. *Environment and Planning A: Economy and Space, 53*(7), 1630–1651.

Simmel, G. (1902) 1964. The metropolis and mental life. In K. H. Wolf (Ed.), *The sociology of Georg Simmel* (pp. 409–424). New York, NY: Free Press.

Sloterdijk, P. (2011). *Spheres* (Vol. 3). Los Angeles, CA: Semiotext (e).

Smith, N. (2005). *The new urban frontier: Gentrification and the revanchist city.* New York, NY: Routledge.

Smith, A. (2012). *Events and urban regeneration: The strategic use of events to revitalise cities.* Routledge.

Smith, L. T. (2012). *Decolonizing methodologies: Research and indigenous peoples.* London: Zed Books.

Thambinathan, V., & Kinsella, E. A. (2021). Decolonizing methodologies in qualitative research: Creative spaces for transformative Praxis. *International Journal of Qualitative Methods, 20*(1). doi:10.1177/16094069211014766

Therborn, G. (2017). *Cities of power: The urban, the national, the popular, the global.* London: Verso Books.

Topak, Ö. E. (2019). Humanitarian and human rights surveillance: The challenge to border surveillance and invisibility? *Surveillance and Society, 17*(3/4), 382–404.

Urry, J. (2012). *Sociology beyond societies: Mobilities for the twenty-first century.* London: Routledge.

Urry, J., & Larsen, J. (2011). *The tourist gaze 3.0.* New York, NY: Sage.

Wekker, G. (2016). *White innocence: Paradoxes of colonialism and race.* Durham: Duke University Press.

Zukin, S. (1996). *The cultures of cities.* London: Wiley-Blackwell.

Zukin, S. (2012). The social production of urban cultural heritage: Identity and ecosystem on an Amsterdam shopping street. *City, Culture and Society, 3*(4), 281–291.

Zukin, S. (2020). Seeing like a city: How tech became urban. *Theory and Society, 49*(5), 941–964.

Chapter 6

FOR AN "EXPANDED" VISUAL/ SENSORY ETHNOGRAPHY: CO-LIVING WITH DEATH IN NEW DELHI[1]

Paolo Silvio Harald Favero

ABSTRACT

The present chapter explores the topic of death in the context of contemporary New Delhi, India. Building upon what I chose to call an 'expanded ethnography', it explores the multiple ways in which sensory, visual and digital mediations and tools can help researchers address such an existentially delicate topic. Building on a mix of online visual ethnography (of computer screens and smartphones), of bodily/sensory practices, of sound recording and image-making, my research focussed on retirement homes and shelters amidst a bulging Indian metropolis. I engaged with subjects who, because of personal choices or family difficulties, have ended up finishing their lives in solitude amidst a city forced to co-live with the presence of death. Alternating between photographic portraits, filmic observations and moments of playful exchanges in front of a camera (with me as one of the objects portrayed) my method capitalizes upon the integration (and problematisation) of bodily (sensory and affective) as well as digital techniques. All together these different mediations have granted me access to different layers of connection to the topic of death in Delhi and also to my ageing guides/interlocutors.

---

[1]I acknowledge Siddhart Pachisa, Roberto Anchisi and Luc Pauwels for endless inspiration. The text is dedicated to Sri Ravi Kalra.

Visual and Multimodal Urban Sociology, Part B
Research in Urban Sociology, Volume 18B, 143–170
Copyright © 2023 by Emerald Publishing Limited
ISSN: 1047-0042/doi:10.1108/S1047-00422023000018B006

Keywords: Death; India; visual ethnography; sensory ethnography; smartphone ethnography; arts-based research; multimodality; existential anthropology

1. OPENING VIGNETTE

One night, many years ago, a friend of mine, I will call him Arjun, was driving home drunk after a party. Suddenly, on a flyover, he felt the car bumping, as if he had driven over something. Confused by the drunken state of his mind he quickly looked back and saw something lying on the street. Not sure what it was (It could have been a carcass, or maybe a bag of jute fallen off from one on the many transports that cross Delhi at night) he decided to drive further. The morning after, on a bad hangover, he read in the news that a man had been killed on the same flyover he had driven on. The deceased was one of the many migrant workers who sleep on the city pavements at night waiting for a bus or for a truck offering them a day wage. He had been killed while crossing the road. Guided by his sense of justice, Arjun decided to go to the police. He described the event he had witnessed to in the presence of a local constable. A report was written and filed, and from that moment onwards, a long period of uncertainty started for him. Progressively pushed against the wall by corrupted policemen, he ended up using his savings for avoiding the worst consequences of his act. He bribed them, several of them. Nevertheless, he ended up in court, accused of manslaughter. The coming months became unbearably hard for him. He went in and out of legal courts and police stations, praying for a chance to redeem himself, while accepting the inevitability of what the judges might eventually decide. Due to a set of unexpected circumstances the judge in charge of the case got eventually dismissed. The new judge, a young man with little experience, got immediately suspicious of the doings of his predecessor. He reopened the case. He called back all the witnesses, looked at all evidence available, enquired also into the bribes that had surrounded the case etc. And eventually he found Arjun innocent. The events were clear. And they had apparently been so for quite some time. Yet, due to the number of people involved in the bribing, nothing had really sipped out. My friend had indeed driven over a man. Yet, according to witnesses that had previously been silenced, the corpse of a man had been seen being thrown off a truck by a car just minutes (possibly seconds?) before Arjun drove past. So, Arjun had not killed anyone. He had driven over the body of a dead man.

2. INTRODUCTION

In this story, which is part of my ethnography in and on Delhi, one important figure is missing. That is the dead man. Both in the news as well as in the debates that followed (in the news as well as among my interlocutors), his name was never mentioned. His role appears, in fact, in the unfolding of the events tangential. Sadly enough, events such as this one happen quite often in Delhi. People (always the poor ones) get killed by over-speeding cars while waiting for a bus, while

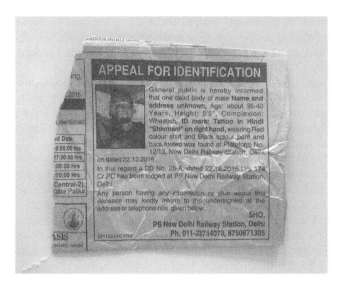

Fig. 1.   Appeal for Identification Appearing in an Indian Daily. *Source:*
Photo by Paolo Silvio Harald Favero.

sleeping on a sidewalk or while crossing the road.[2] Yet this even also testifies to something more – to the fact that death is banal in Delhi; it is an accepted part of life.

Delhi's inhabitants (the Dilliwhallas) just co-exist with death in fact. They don't make a fuss about its evident presence. Death is a constitutive part of the everyday life of this city and it reaches its inhabitants in a variety of (silent or loud) ways. It can be spotted in the shape of corpses of animals lying on a sidewalk, or in the eyes of the many homeless people sleeping on the side of a road. For the poor, Delhi is an eternal battleground. You just need to drive past the station at night and notice the number of humans struggling to survive until the day after. Death dances around these bodies and every now and then it takes one of them in her embrace. Yet death can also be loud, blatantly screened in the media. Images of found anonymous corpses awaiting identification decorate the pages of the newspapers (Fig. 1).

---

[2]In 1999, a BMW driving at 140 km/hr killed six people just like that, in a case that eventually managed to shake Delhi's upper-class society. The crash was so violent that bloodstains and parts of the bodies of the victims were found at a radius of 100 metres from the place of the collision. In the car were three young men in their early twenties, driving home drunk from a party. They ran away from the scene and immediately asked their servants to clean the car from any blood stains. All belonging to influential families, the three men were eventually identified. They were first acquitted but one of them eventually got sentenced to two years of prison in 2008. As in the story I narrated above, little attention was given in the news to the six people who died in the accident.

And indeed, in traditional settings the body of the dead is displayed before cremation, paraded on the streets covered only by a thin white veil. White, the resulting amalgam of the fusions of all colours and the symbol of light, is the hue of death here.

Yet, at the same time, death crawls also silently and viciously into the bodies of Delhi's inhabitants under the safe disguise of fresh air. Every day spent in this city shortens your life with one hour they say. The air is just as polluted as the water. Delhi is truly delhi-rious. Like writer Kushwant Singh once wrote: 'In Delhi, death and drink make life worth living'.

My recent fieldwork in Delhi explores this terrain. Starting with an interest for the role of aesthetics in experiences of death, loss and grief, my research progressively geared towards a sensory, affective and existential exploration of death in Delhi. In my work I consciously experimented with a variety of different (audio/visual/sensory) techniques and tools to investigate how human beings who are preparing themselves for the final passage cope with the moment. Jumping across online and offline worlds, I explored the various ways in which ageing, or diseased or otherwise challenged human beings mediate this experience; the poetics of their reflections, the sources from which they gather them. They are my 'guides' into this process, not my 'informants'.

And indeed, India (and not just Delhi) offers a particularly interesting terrain for a scholar (especially an anthropologist) interested in death. Stereotypically this is a 'spiritual' civilisation that for a large part of its population also believes in reincarnation. Circularity and continuity (supposedly) characterise the Indian approach to death. This is what we generally believe, and this is what I wanted to test with my research. Conducting fieldwork I discovered, eventually, how for most of my elder interlocutors, death and aging were not particularly relevant subjects. They were just part of everyday life. They lovingly, compassionately co-lived with it.

Underpinning my research project is a specific interest for Delhi, the city on which I have my key expertise as an anthropologist and a place that I consider to be a true adoptive home. This metropolis, capital of India, constitutes for my work more than a field, a space, a venue hosting my fieldwork. Delhi is to me a true longitudinal object of work and life since the late 1990s. My new research marks my desire to re-discover it and to enter it from a new angle. And indeed, this new angle is crafted vis-à-vis my personal life trajectory. My arrival to Delhi in 2019 was the ending point of a long journey, an introspective search on the topic of death, grief and aging that started with the passing away of my father in 2015. I came to Delhi on a sabbatical break to reconnect the dots. To bring my personal story of grief, loss and separation (that had turned into an insistent exercise in auto-ethnography and storytelling, cf. Favero, 2018) into something broader, something to be shared with other individuals. From introspection to extrospection following Tagore's lesson that becoming yourself is something that you have to do in company. Through my own story I wanted to reach out to other subjects and connect with their ways of dealing with grief, separation and death. I explored not only the 'know-able' but also the 'be-able'.

The key point in this chapter is to look into the various ways through which I attempted to connect with death during my work in Delhi. These range from online searches to the use of smartphone apps to sensory practices, sound recording and image-making. Together they granted me access to different layers of understanding of the meaning of death. During my research I embraced what I call an 'expanded' ethnographic approach. I borrow the metaphor of expansion from the world of physics,[3] where it stands for a volumetric movement. An expansion is not linear, it does not aim at sticking events together in cause-and-effect relations. Expansion is gaseous and moves in all directions, hence opening up the terrain for serendipitous encounters. More concretely, my method is characterised by the simultaneous use (and problematisation) of bodily (sensory and affective) as well as digital techniques. I alternated moments of simple being and presencing in the habitats within which I chose to do research with more detailed audio/visual explorations, with interviews and participatory activities. I critically exploit the capacity of my senses to contemplate the world surrounding me, addressing the extent to which digital tools can compensate the flaws and limits of bodily perceptions. I extensively incorporated the smartphone, the camera and the sound recorder as portals to the worlds I was investigating. I kept recording short videos (I call them video postcards) of the places where I went to. I filmed from the cars and three-wheelers as I travelled across the city. I recorded soundscapes. I took selfies, also in company of the elders that I conducted research with. I used my phone for staying in touch with my interlocutors, for sharing pictures, songs and messages with them. This is the tool that we use for staying in touch today too. A way to be present even when absent. Condensing personal and group messages, photos and sounds, gifs, news, maps and personal notes, the smartphone became a key tool for exploring my ways of experiencing the role and meaning of death in Delhi. I used it when writing this chapter remembering the moments that characterised my stay in Delhi. In writing this chapter I have in fact built my story in the review mirror, looking back at all the images sounds and written notes I had stored in there.

I will start my story below with a brief contextualisation of Delhi and its history. I will connect these to my own research trajectory and then, after a short theoretical parenthesis on the meaning of mediation in a post-digital context, shift to discuss the three main waves through which death became a matter of debate in Delhi. Sticking mainly to one of these waves, i.e. the air pollution crisis, I will look into how it entered the lives of my interlocutors and helped me to better get a sense of what death means to them. Doing this I will reflect upon the implications of my methodological choices.

3. ABOUT DELHI

Delhi is no neutral place to me, nor is it for most of its visitors or inhabitants. This is where I had done most of my work as an anthropologist and an

---

[3]Thanks Cristina Favero for helping me clarify the meaning of this metaphor in physics.

image-maker. I first came to Delhi in 1995 as a backpacker. I came back in 1997 for a four-month fieldwork in a mental hospital located in Shahdhara, one of its suburbs, and I then lived here between 1998 and 2001 for my PhD fieldwork on young middle- and upper-class men. My engagement with the city went on with a new project on image-makers and politics which resulted, after nearly 15 years of research, in my latest book (Favero, 2020). Now, as mentioned above, I wanted to give my engagement with Delhi a fresh new start and break loose from previous interests, networks and perspectives. I wanted to learn to look at the city that I had in the past explored as a meeting point of transcultural flows (Favero, 2003, 2005) through a different lens, that of the co-existence with death.

Most foreign visitors tend to despise Delhi. Tourists only 'use' it as a stopover on their way elsewhere. While in town, they may visit the Red Fort, Old Delhi and India Gate but they seldom cross the line represented by Rajpath, the ceremonial road on which India Gate is located, hence missing out on all the beautiful parks and forests that South Delhi has to offer. Delhi, as Bhatia (1994) suggested long ago, can be seen as an 'urban gallery', an 'architectural canvas on public display' (p. 32). Its architecture displays the various epochs in which it has been built. It incorporates the colonial and the postmodern, the Mughal and the Hindu, the modernism of the 1960s and 1970s and the famous 'Punjabi Baroque' (Bhatia, 1994). And it speaks of its monumental instinct, its intrinsic desire for greatness. Delhi has been the battleground for many powers and the capital of seven empires (cf. Jain, 1990). This has resulted it into a unique blend of Hindu, Muslim and Western cultural influences. And today it is critically being rebuilt as the capital of yet another empire, the one that Prime Minister Modi is attempting to build under the banner of Hinduism.

A metropolis containing not only palaces but also amazing gardens, forests and urban villages (i.e. proper rural areas contained by the city), Delhi has inspired writers and poets across the epochs. Kushwant Singh, whom I already mentioned above, compares Delhi to his beloved transvestite prostitute Bhagmati:

> They have two things in common: they are lots of fun. And they are sterile…Having been long misused by rough people they have learnt to conceal their seductive charms under a mask of repulsive ugliness. (Singh, 1990:30 and p. 1)

Testifying to its ambivalent character, contemporary poet Amit Dahiyabadshah (one of my field interlocutors) says that Delhi is 'an imperial city with the flavours of a village'. Many poets have praised the beauty of Delhi: 'these are not the streets of Delhi but the canvas of an artist' wrote eighteenth century Mir Taqi Mir. And many its ugliness: 'city that the heavens have looted and laid waste' said Asaf-ud-Daula (Nawab of Oudh, eighteenth century). The poets are indeed right. Delhi is all of this. It is immense beauty but also smell of defeat decay and death; Delhi is 'a city of love' (twentieth century poet Bashir Badri).

So, Delhi has a paradoxical double nature, a co-existence of grandeur and decadence, of life and death. I believe that the Kantian notion of the sublime, that ungraspable blend of fear and beauty that characterises the view of an avalanche falling from a mountain, manages to render the sense of the experience of Delhi.

'The world is the body and Delhi is its soul' wrote Delhi poet Mirza Ghalib (1797–1869) voicing the centrality of what today is India's capital and its capacity to melt together such a great variety of influences.

Upon starting my new phase of research, I had to do an act of estrangement in and from Delhi. I had to decentre my own point of view on the city that I loved and spent so much time in. In a way I had to make the same effort that ethnographers make when studying 'at home' (Abu-Lughod, 1991; Naraya, 1993). But after all, this is what an anthropologist should be, a 'professional stranger' (Agar, 1996). For doing this I alternated between different approaches and techniques, trying to always leave room for novelty, for the unexpected (hence avoiding projecting my previous understanding of the city and of the topic under scrutiny). I tried exercising what Stoller (1989) calls 'epistemological humility'. My technique was to alternate my attention to the senses (hence focussing on sound, touch, smell, vision, spatial awareness and introception) with the accumulation of often unpretentious (visual and sonic) impressions taken on my smartphone and by juxtaposing insights gathered from online and offline spaces. I tried foregrounding intuition, serendipity, and, challenging Geertz (1973), the 'thin' rather than the 'thick' (cf. also Favero, 2017). A case, perhaps, of conscious 'epistemological superficiality'.

Online, I mapped organisations, associations and homes that were devoted to the care of the elders. I also used 'Google Trends' to identify hot topics, looked at visualizations of data etc. But indeed, I also followed conventional mass media, such as television and newspapers, and supported my search also by exploring connections through people I already knew (the result was, however, never as good as with the organisations that I found online). On top of it I read a lot of poetry, another precious portal to culturally situated narratives on aging and death. Through my reconnaissance I ended up selecting three venues for my research. The first one is a middle/upper-class residence for paying senior citizens (I will call it Mokshdhamas). The second, a smaller NGO-run shelter for 12–15 individuals in need of help. And the latter is a large shelter in the outskirts of Delhi with around 500 residents (I will call it TGF, The Great Foundation). Some young but most of them old, these individuals have been rescued from the streets.

In parallel to this more goal-oriented search, I also tried to explore the various connections with death that the city displays visually, sensorially. I got inspired to re-enact an exercise that I had done a few years earlier while in Hiroshima, Japan. Less than a year after my father's death, I found myself in the city that more than any other place possibly represents death and especially human-inflicted death. It was a grey rainy day when Luc Pauwels and I decided to spend some time walking around the city with our cameras. We took as usual separate routes and gave each other appointment after a couple of hours by the Hiroshima Dome, the only building that survived the atomic explosion. During my walk, I photographed in a spontaneous, responsive way. I did not plan to 'capture', 'document' or 'represent' death as it appeared there. I did not try to attribute meaning. I focussed on the 'be-able' not on the 'know-able' and let myself get guided by intuition, using the camera more as a compass, a tool guiding my exploration than a tool for narrating and explaining what I already had in mind. I was hoping in that way that I could allow the greyness and sadness of Hiroshima to find an original way into my camera (and my consciousness) and that they could enter my own world on their own terms hence offering me possibly another insight on death. So, I walked around making pictures 'aimlessly' (Favero, 2013), seren-dipitously, whenever something attracted me. Basically, I responded with the camera to what grabbed, for a reason or another, my attention. I photographed the tourists by the dome; the grey waves forming on top of the river and the droplets of rain morphing the view of the memorial from behind a glass window. As anticipated above, in each of these places I photographed in an intuitive modality that foregrounded the 'mimetic' rather than the 'expressive' (Pauwels, 2015). I did not think about the possible outcome of my work and the use I could make of my images. The camera was an extension of my body, the mediator of my exploration, my guide. Similarly, to what I had done before in exploring my father's death (Favero, 2018), I approached it as a tool for becoming, for opening up time and for being in the world rather than for 'slicing', 'capturing' and then re-presenting it.[4] Once back to my hotel room that night I put down the camera bag without even looking at my images. Tired and happy after a good dinner with Luc, I decided to leave that for the day after. Looking at the images on my laptop in the morning I was met by a surprise. Instead of death I had found life. In each of the images that I remembered as messengers of sadness, greyness and death, I now saw signs of joy, of light and life. A happily flying seagull breaks the grey geometry of waves on the river overlooking the dome; an old lady lovingly holds the umbrella over her husband's head as he makes a photograph of the dome; a red-clad woman flushes a rainy alley with her colour; and finally, a young woman stretching up her umbrella interrupts a cupola of umbrellas that seemed to counterpoint rhetorically the dome on which the bomb had fallen (Fig. 2). On her arm a wristwatch is visible, signalling the passing of time, as life goes on. In these photographs, I had found life amidst my search for death. In Hiroshima, the camera/compass/guide brought to my attention a different view than the one that fitted the narrative that I, merging history with my story (Gramsci, 2007[1971]), had consolidated in my awareness about Hiroshima. Interrupting the 'herme-neutic circle' (Albers & James, 1988), the camera became a tool for seeing anew. Paraphrasing MacDougall (1997), it did not show things in a different way but really pointed me towards new things to look at and understand.

Once in Delhi, I enacted a similar search and explored signs of death in the city. Compared to Hiroshima, the scope of my research was now obviously both broader and more precise. My working experience too, with different kinds of (technological and bodily) mediations, had now become greater. And as described earlier, here I also combined the use of tools and techniques for research online with those for conducting audio–visual–sensory research. This

---

[4]In fact, I cherish the co-existence of the two dimensions in a photograph. Its capacity to foreground simultaneously both presence and performance and realist representation. And in my vocabulary, photographs are 'made' not 'taken'.

Fig. 2. Hiroshima's Life. *Source:* Photo by Paolo Silvio Harald Favero.

'expanded' ethnographic method quickly pointed me in the direction of a number of key topics that strongly influenced the way in which death was experienced in Delhi. I will get back to this right after a short theoretical preamble.

4. ETHNOGRAPHY IN AN 'EXPANDED' TERRAIN

As mentioned above, the first entry into my field was indeed from a 'macro' perspective. I tried looking at the big picture. Despite aiming at entering the lives of specific individuals, I started by mapping the terrain of death in/and Delhi by means of a variety of technologies and techniques, touching both (and bringing in dialogue) online and offline worlds. I suggest that this is today a necessity. Life in urban contexts is made up by a subtle blend of information, sensations and perceptions that reach us simultaneously via our bodies and via a variety of technologies of mediation. With the latter term I imply all possible tools and materials that mediate our multiple relations to the world that surrounds us. No matter whether by elements belonging to the digital or to the 'terrane' order (Byung-Chul Han, 2022), our ways of being in the world are always mediated. From the skin to the eye (Lehmuskallio, 2019), to spectacles, contact lenses, hearing aids and the variety of contemporary digital tools that many citizens use today when moving in a city, we are wrapped in mediations (and through them in relations). Technologies, no matter whether digital or otherwise, must be considered as simple prolongations of bodies. They are prosthesis, McLuhan

(1994) suggested long ago. They extend (or better, expand) our reach into the world.

In this scenario it makes little sense to pull the digital and the analogue apart from each other. This is just a long circular continuum, where elements remand back to each other. It probably makes better sense today to talk about the post-digital, a terrain where the digital and the non-digital meet and merge blurring their opposition (and the dualisms attached) while crafting our experiences. Following the same logic, it also makes little sense to maintain the idea of the digital as a terrain of immateriality and disembodiment. In line with other scholars (among them Hine, 2015; Horst & Miller, 2012), I believe that the digital today defines and encapsulates our very humanity. It is not in opposition to it. The concreteness of the digital is observable at many levels. On first level is that of the materiality of its infrastructure, of the heavy structures that support digital communication systems. I am thinking here of the sheer size and weight of the premises hosting Apple's Cloud, or of the quantity of cables of all sorts that fill our homes, and of the ever-growing amount of e-waste that accumulates in the oceans and landfills of the world. Secondly, beyond the concrete, metal and wood surfaces that make up the material infrastructure of our cities, there lies also another layer of infrastructure made up of Wi-Fi and Bluetooth fields, flows of information directed by GPS and microwave signals. Less visible at first sight, this infrastructure conditions however our behaviour in a significant way. It is material insofar as it literally puts us in motion redesigning also the spaces in which we live. I just need to reflect on the ticket I got last month for following blindly my GPS tracker in a one-way street to realise this. Think also of those smartphone applications that interact materially with their users. This can be the case of the many COVID safe apps that take note (via Bluetooth technology) of the people you encounter, hence allowing medical personnel to trace you up if you would have come too close to someone who tested positive[5] or of the dating apps informing you about the presence of someone from the same community in physical space, hence promoting the passage from virtual to physical contact. Albeit not directly observable, Bluetooth signals are concrete, material and visible in the behaviours that they generate. And the same can also be said about Wi-Fi signal. That too is not directly observable, but it can be visualised by means of heat maps for instance. Its presence or absence reveals precious information on urban space pointing out economic gaps. And indeed, with a degree of creativity Wi-Fi signal can be photographed too. A group of artists and scholars from the Oslo School of Management and Design has managed to combine light painting and Wi-Fi signal strength detectors and generate visualisation of Wi-Fi signal in urban environments.

In my work in Cuba, I have witnessed the transformative power of Wi-Fi from the point of view of urban design. The insertion of Wi-Fi signal (distributed perhaps only informally by one of the many 'el commodify', i.e. the semi-legal signal vendors) has contributed in morphing the face of particular parts of cities

---

[5]https://www.health.gov.au/resources/apps-and-tools/covidsafe-app.

such as Havana and Santiago. Anonymous street corners have become real hubs attracting not only Wi-Fi clients but also vendors of snacks and drinks, while next-door beautiful (but non-connected) parks have developed into abandoned and sometimes dangerous areas. The presence or absence of Wi-Fi or Bluetooth signal can also offer us a precious indicator of class relations in a city. Think of the maps generated by users of fitness apps. Strava's Global Heatmap condenses in images that can be seen online the data produced by its users. Some years ago, this site became the object of a major scandal because its images, displaying data produced by its users, also displayed online the position and movement of US soldiers, hence 'giving away' the location of secret US army bases in Afghanistan, Syria and Djibouti.

Looking at a map of Delhi through Strava's heatmaps, a viewer can identify the accessibility and possibly also the income levels of different parts of the city. The map displays in bright colours the routes (and hence the areas contained by them) with more users. These have evidently better, runner-friendly infrastructure and parks, which makes us assume also that they can be used as indicators of social class and generic wealth. Just focus on the centre of the map below. There is a dark area under which you can see two circles. The dark part is Old Delhi an urban planner's nightmare; a congested area with high population density, traffic and pollution. The light spots are Rajpat and the areas around India Gate, the greenest part of Delhi where also politicians and other influential people reside.

In such a scenario, and especially in metropolitan contexts, we must evidently abandon old-fashioned distinctions between material and immaterial, mediated and non-mediated. Let us rather look at our ways of being in the world as increasingly positioned along a continuum that goes from purely bodily to digitally mediated perceptions. We live today in this co-existence of dimensions, an expanded terrain that requires an 'expanded ethnographic' approach (Fig. 3).

Fig. 3. Delhi Heat Map. *Source:* Screenshot by Paolo Silvio Harald Favero from https://www.strava.com/heatmap#4.00/-120.90000/38.36000/hot/all.

5. THREE WAVES OF DYING

Looking into my smartphone as a field diary, the first picture I encounter from my arrival to Delhi in 2019 is that of a foggy runaway (Fig. 4). Landing on an early November day the sky looked like a pink/orange sticky foam. The poisonous air wrapped me in as the plane moved towards the airport. I felt it crawling into my lungs as I stepped out. In fact, I have always loved that smell upon landing in Delhi. A difficultly defined blend of tempting scents and decaying materials. Stepping off the plane most people covered their mouths with a handkerchief (another common thing to see in the city). The better organised ones had masks (and this is before the arrival of COVID-19). I did not cover my face, happy to take in the poison that Delhi had to offer. Quintessential to my state of arousal for being there.

Pollution is, sadly enough, a (significant) part of what Delhi is. This is one of the most polluted cities in the world (probably the most polluted one). 54 Thousands people died in the capital city in 2020 due to PM2.5 (the fine particulate matter smaller than 2.5 micrometres in diameter). To breathe in Delhi's air, says one recent report, is like smoking 44 cigarettes a day.[6] The air pollutant particles in Delhi are almost six times higher than the maximum limit prescribed by the World Health Organization (WHO).[7] So as European cities go on alert at 60 or 80 AQI (Air Quality Index), when I landed in Delhi the reported value was, according to AirVisual, at 570. I had reached Delhi during a major wave of pollution, a moment that heightened the debates around the deadliness and poisonous character of this city. AirVisual is one of the smartphone applications that Delhiites use for guiding their pollution-related behaviour. Similar digital tools have become a key affordance for surviving in Delhi. During cold winter days (when pollution reaches its highest peak), the concentration of PM2.5 is so high that children are not allowed to go out and hence not even to school. AirVisual is adopted not only by anxious parents but also, for instance, by sports people who try to figure out whether and when they can train. AirVisual provides another kind visualisation of Delhi, a map of its toxicity, indicating the places with better or worst air. The app also gives recommendations as to the kinds of activities that can be conducted (including opening the windows at home).

Air is therefore a scarce resource in Delhi, or rather, it is a toxic resource. The mouth mask, that most citizens of the world have discovered during the peaks of the COVID-19 pandemic, have for long been part of the prevention campaigns ran by Delhi's government. Yet, most citizens do not seem to bother much. Very few use the mask in public defying the evident risks (another sign of the capacity to co-exist with death). Yet, middle- or upper-class families have become quite conscious about the quality of the air in their homes. Domestic air pollution filters are today one of the top-selling home appliances. Clearing the air from

---

[6]https://edition.cnn.com/2017/11/10/health/delhi-pollution-equivalent-cigarettes-a-day/index.html.
[7]https://www.ndtv.com/delhi-news/over-50-000-people-in-delhi-died-due-to-pm2-5-air-pollution-last-year-study-2373223.

Fig. 4.   Delhi Landing. *Source:* Photo by Paolo Silvio Harald Favero.

PM2.5, these tools are placed in every environment of the house and incorporated in the AC system of most medium and high-end cars. This is a key appliance for the well-to-do, and I have seen on so many occasions friends exchanging suggestions on the best machines to purchase, their design etc. Anyway, in my room in Delhi I often measured values above 150 with my fancy Philips air filter with its multicolour lights (Fig. 5). The need to filter the air is just in line with that of filtering the water. Both are poisonous and scarce.

There is another paradox here. Counter-intuitively, clean air in Delhi is the result of closed windows and good air purifiers. It is the result of the intervention of culture (technology) and not nature. And this human gesture also strengthens the public–private divide. In an Indian urban context, the very idea of the 'public' is historically a contested one. It entered India during the British era, together with that of the 'modern city'. Symbolic of the British presence, the 'public' was an 'orderly, hygienic, scientific, technologically superior, and "civilized"' space (Kaviraj, 1997, p. 84) within which colonial administrators could exercise control over the territory. The idea of a regulated 'public space' (in opposition to the 'private') was hence invested with negative associations from the very beginning. Whatever was external to the house became, from colonial times onwards, treated as a kind of non-space, 'an empty, valueless negative of the private' (p. 105) for which no individuals or communities had any clear, well-defined responsibility or obligation. The debate on the air quality falls perfectly in line with this

Fig. 5.   My Air Filter. *Source:* Photo by Paolo Silvio Harald Favero.

distinction. The negative association has been so deeply ingrained that one campaign against death penalty used the sentence 'It is important that air quality of Delhi NCR is worst and it's like a gas chamber…then why death penalty?'[8]

Delhi's Chief Minister Arvind Kejriwal (who during one interview also called Delhi 'a gas chamber') has attempted to act against the pollution levels in the city. He guided the construction of 'smog towers', gigantic air filters placed in crucial parts of the city that are today looked upon as the only hope for the future survival of Delhi (Fig. 6).

I too experienced the toxicity of the urban environment at a variety of levels. From my dirty nostril and my permanent cough to my use of AirVisual and other digital visualisations to organise my day. Google Trends, a tool that can extensively be used to grasp a sense of the geographical distribution of key debates on the planet, also gave me an interesting overview. According to this search engine, the topic 'Air pollution' is mostly searched in Nepal and India comes in the sixth place. But on a search for 'Air pollution filters' India is the leading country, long before the United States. With all their relativity, such online research tools provide an orientation and a first mapping of topics that are relevant at local level.

I witnessed to two more waves of death during my stay in Delhi. The second wave was political in nature and came as the result of the introduction of the Citizenship Amendment Act. On December 11th, 2019, the Parliament of India amended a 1955 law, offering members of persecuted religious minorities from Afghanistan, Bangladesh and Pakistan who have lived in India since December

---

[8]http://timesofindia.indiatimes.com/articleshow/72464051.cms?
utm_source=contentofinterest&utm_medium=text&utm_campaign=cppst.

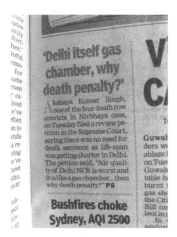

Fig. 6.   Delhi is a Death Chamber. *Source:* Photo by Paolo Silvio Harald
Favero.

2014 the right to apply for Indian citizenship. The discriminatory character of this
act resides in the fact that the amendment applies only to Hindus, Sikhs, Bud-
dhists, Jains, Parsis and Christians. No mention is made of Muslims. Called by
the BBC as 'India's new "anti-Muslim" law',[9] the act triggered off vehement
reactions all over India. After a period of peaceful protests (in December) the
month of February brought along a wave of terror. In the Northeast of Delhi,
beginning on the 23rd of February 2020, a scene that had been already seen in so
many different parts of India (and notably in Gujarat, 2002, see Favero, 2020)
was re-enacted: Hindu mobs attacking Muslim households, shops and mosques.
In what appeared to be an organised action rather than, as state and media
defined it, a 'riot', or a 'spontaneous' upsurge of violence, Hindu activists set
mosques on fire, brutalised men and raped the women. 53 people died (more than
two-thirds of them being Muslim). These tensions affected indeed my fieldwork.
Partly they affected the mood of many of my interlocutors (despite their varied
views on Indian politics), but they also caused disruptions in my movements and
my communications with the elders. To silence the protests, the areas where
demonstrators gathered got digitally sealed off by the police. The city turned into
the worst jam ever. With maps, online transportation services (such as Uber, Ola
etc.), WhatsApp etc. being (in certain areas) suspended, fieldwork became a
complicated issue. And as Muslim neighbourhoods in Northeast Delhi were still
burning, news started reaching India about the possible arrival of COVID-19. A
third wave of death awareness had begun, and I remember sitting watching TV at
night at home in Delhi, looking at the figures of raising cases in Europe, hearing
stories of people getting hospitalised and dying in Italy and Belgium. COVID
seemed, at that point, however, to be less dangerous than the angry Hindu mobs

---

[9]https://www.bbc.com/news/world-asia-india-50670393.

not far from where I lived. Watching the television at night, me and my friend
Rohit could just not put the events together. The presence of death just a few
neighbourhoods away from us was so much more tangible than the news coming
in from the world. Also, we got more upset about Trump's official visit in India
than by COVID itself. Adding to the cynicism of the present Indian government,
Modi had in fact welcomed Trump parading him across the streets of Agra and
Ahmedabad after having made sure that walls were built in vicinity of slums with
its starving individuals. As Modi tried to make the poor invisible, death made
itself visible in many other shapes during those days.

6. BACK INTO THE EVERYDAY

These three waves of death did obviously bounce back upon my research practice. Each one became part of some of the exchanges I had with my interlocutors.
Pollution, the topic that I will unpack further here, struck down, as an issue,
during one of my morning walks with a man that I call, following his wish, Slimy
Sid. A 75-year-old gentleman who decided (at the age of 70) to free himself from
all responsibilities and belongings and to leave a successful company in the hands
of his children, Slimy Sid, lives in the more high-end retirement home that I
mentioned briefly at the beginning, Mokshdhamas. Located in one of Delhi's
former urban 'villages', this is a small haven for senior citizens. It is a private
structure where guests can each have their own room and access to several
facilities: a dining hall (with vegetarian meals served for breakfast, lunch and
dinner), an open kitchen (for those who may prefer a non-veg diet); a garden; a
meeting room (hosting activities) and importantly a rooftop terrace. It is on this
rooftop terrace that I used to meet Slimy Sid on an almost daily basis. Often, we
met in the morning lights. And it was during such an early November day that me
and my camera joined him for a walk around the flowery central courtyard (Fig.
7). I pointed as usual the camera towards me and Slimy Sid, this time filming us
as we walked. It was my habit, in Mokshdhamas in other places, to always keep
the camera with me, re-enacting MacDougall's idea of being a man with the
movie camera. When I look at myself during those long moments of exploration,
I experience my body as a prothesis of the camera rather than the other way
around. I become the object of my own explorations being part of the scenes that
the camera portrays (and produces). In conversation with Slimy Sid, I become
also another kind of object, the object of his care and compassion (not the other
way around). This morning walk provided me with two precious insights. The
first one relates to the fear of the effects of pollution and Slimy Sid's acceptance of
its presence in his life. The air quality of winter mornings in Delhi is always
particularly bad. This is when the accumulation of particles is the highest.
Mornings collect the result of the trucks driving through the city during the night,
of the commuters going to work in the morning and of the smoke of all the fires
lit up by street dwellers in need to keep them warm. And indeed, smoke is bad for
vulnerable subjects such as an aging man whose life has been a rollercoaster. That
morning I asked Slimy Sid if he was confident in walking and he commented with

Fig. 7. Still Frame of Slimy Sid and Paolo Walking. *Source:* Filming by
Paolo Silvio Harald Favero.

a degree of positivity that he believed that the air was fine in that moment; it was
good because it is good 'as long as you're not choking', he said. Generally, he told
me, he would cough all the time coming up here in the morning. Now it felt okay.
His comment, spurred by our chatting about the weather, showed the high level
of acceptance Slimy Sid, like many Delhi inhabitants, have for the situation.
Unbothered by the risk of lung diseases, most people still go out to do their
exercise, just like Slimy Sid during this beautiful morning. They calmly co-live
with the risk of dying.

Suddenly, during our walk, I put the camera down on a tripod, filming the two
of us walking around the central opening of the terrace from a low diagonal
angle. This led to another insight. Walking interviews, such as the one I conducted here with Slimy Sid, are very useful to connect and to let topics emerge
spontaneously. With the body being busy moving and the mind floating around
attracted simultaneously by all the senses, the researcher is given an opportunity
to explore the poetics of the research participants. As Ingold said '[l]ocomotion,
not cognition, must be the starting point for the study of perceptual activity'
(Ingold, 2004, p. 331). In walking, especially in outdoor spaces, all the senses
come together: perception (smell, touch and hearing) merge with proprioception
(movement), introception (the feeling of what goes on inside of us) and ther-
moception (the perception of temperature). To use a reference to Indian cos-
mology, walking makes us connect with the five elements: earth, fire, air, water
and space/ether. These elements correspond also to different sense organs (ears,
skin, eyes, tongue and nose). The latter element, i.e. ether, or space, is, however,
the most interesting one. According to Tibetan Buddhism, this is the last element
we abandon when we die. And for the neurosciences today, the perception of
space (or spatiality) is the one connected to the functions of the non-linguistic,

part of the brain, to the 'non-interpretive mind' (Niebauer, 2019). This part dominates the process of spatial processing and acts like a kind of background within which all other elements are allowed to appear. This volumetric consciousness comes to the fore, for instance, when meditating and also when walking. When walking we are in fact, as researchers, not only given an opportunity to enter, and be empathetic with, the world of our interlocutors but to also position ourselves within their experiential and perceptual room. With a camera pointed at us, and with compassionated subjects engaging with us, we become the object of our own observations.

Slimy Sid's combination of wittiness and acceptance of life shines through in the materials produced during these walks. Yet these walking conversations also reveal something more subtle, something relational and corporal that occurred to me (the researcher) rather than to him (the research participant). Turn after turn in the garden terrace, my body lets progressively go of the stress, the tensions and the preoccupations of my own lifeworld. Like a disciple in the presence of a guru I progressively slow down, letting Slimy Sid's pace take over. On the video filmed with the camera positioned on a small tripod on the floor, I can see my feet gliding on the floor (just like Slimy Sid does). My posture looks progressively, by every turn of the central courtyard, more relaxed. Despite the seriousness of our conversations, a smile finds room on my face and on his (Fig. 8).

One of the strongest impressions that I have from the time spent at Mokshdhamas is that feeling of slowing down each time I entered this space (and especially Slimy Sid's existential space). Outside the chaos of an urbanised village in South Delhi (Fig. 9), inside the peace of men and women who have accepted the passing of time and who daily cultivate their love for life (Fig. 10).

Fig. 8.   Still Frame of Slimy Sid and Paolo Smiling. *Source:* Filming by Paolo Silvio Harald Favero.

Fig. 9.   Still Frame of the Street Facing Mokshdhamas. *Source:* Filming by
Paolo Silvio Harald Favero.

Entering here Slimy Sid stripped himself of all his belongings. He came to
prepare for his death and unburden his family from his presence. Living in a
small room, with white walls, one icon of Krishna (that was there before he
arrived) and a fan hanging from the roof, Slimy Sid did not carry into this place
anything belonging to his past. He came in only with his clothes and his iPad.
'This is my link to the world', he told me once, 'the rest I don't need, the

Fig. 10.   Still Frame of Mokshdhamas. *Source:* Filming by Paolo Silvio
Harald Favero.

memories are vivid in my mind, I just need to close my eyes to see them'. Slimy Sid had to do quite lot of labour to do to adapt to this new life. But now he is in a good place, he says. And he does not fear death; 'this is the last great experience of my life and I want to live to its fullest', he once told me. So, Sid co-exists with it, he accepts it and he almost longs for it. Beyond these words, however, or rather paralleling them, is the calm that emanates from Slimy Sid's way of walking, of talking and of gesticulating. He always takes his time before replying to a comment or answering to a question. Like a meditation teacher, he puts an empty space, a gap, between the words, between action and interpretation. He gives himself (and the listener) time to take things in. And this calm slowly crawls into me. Words fail to communicate this experience. They reduce the 'be-able' to the 'know-able'. They extinguish the embodied and affective state of mind that I experienced. Images are better suited than words to express the inexpressible. They are better suited for expressing the way in which Slimy Sid co-inhabits this space with death while being compassionate, sharing love and warmth. To date, Slimy Sid and I keep sharing images, sounds, affections and words. We communicate almost daily on WhatsApp co-presencing in such a way into each other's lives. Today I am sending him my latest materials filmed with the drone letting him inspire my approach to them through his comments.

Before I conclude, let me however add a couple of reflections on my filming methodology. While conducting fieldwork I alternated between a variety of different filming techniques. I generally started exploring the sensory character of an environment by focussing on the 'whole' rather than the detail. I celebrated the camera's capacity to be superficial, to skim over and caress surfaces rather than seeking for explanations and descriptions; 'a caress does not know what it seeks' said Levinas (1987, p. 89). Foregrounding a sense of presencing I used, in these explorations, the camera mostly as a prolongation of my ear rather than of my eye. I avoided using the headphones while filming, hence expanding my attention beyond the limits imposed by the unidirectional mike. Rather than looking for words and verbalized meanings, I allowed myself to follow the sounds coming to me from all possible directions. This is a key quality of sound, it is truly immersive and it wraps us in, depriving us of the capacity to control what we take in and what we exclude. Sound, Chaudhuri says, is 'totally unregulated by the laws of nations, utterly uncontrollable by human beings, completely impervious to our species' wall-building prowess' (Chaudhuri, 2016). Decentring our desire and capacity to control, frame and attribute meaning to what we see, sound can therefore serendipitously take us to unexpected places. Sounds constitute an opening to the world.

Along with the attention to sound, my methodological approach built also on the constant alternation between media. Often, I would stop filming for taking a photograph (Figs. 11, 12 and 13). Commonly, this gesture had mainly a partic-ipatory, connecting value. Many social actors (especially in India) love having pictures taken of them. And a photograph is easy to show immediately, to share through WhatsApp and to take again and again. Portraits made up a large amount of the photography I did while conducting fieldwork. I discussed with the photographed subject how to portray them, getting them to choose the photo

Fig. 11.   Portrait at TGF. *Source:* Photo by Paolo Silvio Harald Favero.

they preferred. Sometimes I sent the final outcome to them (at least to those in possession of a smartphone). Most often than not, however, my interlocutors just enjoyed the process of being photographed, enjoying the act of becoming that portraiture is also made up of.

And indeed alongside the portraits I also made photographs of moments and events occurring. Often containing a story such photographs often await words to fill in the gaps they open up in our imagination (Figs. 14, 15, 16 and 17).

Fig. 12.   Portrait at TGF. *Source:* Photo by Paolo Silvio Harald Favero.

Fig. 13.   Portrait at TGF. *Source:* Photo by Paolo Silvio Harald Favero.

Fig. 14.   Portrait at TGF. *Source:* Photo by Paolo Silvio Harald Favero.

Fig. 15. Portrait at TGF. *Source:* Photo by Paolo Silvio Harald Favero.

Fig. 16. Portrait at TGF. *Source:* Photo by Paolo Silvio Harald Favero.

Fig. 17.   Portrait at TGF. *Source:* Photo by Paolo Silvio Harald Favero.

I also made a series of photographs that I called 'people and their things'. Most individuals ending up in these retirement homes and shelters do not have many belongings. What they have they store jealously. I asked them to share their stories of their favourite belongings and make portraits of that. Based on these images I carried on elicitation interviews, coming to the core of their stories, memories and affections. In Fig. 18 a lady that I shall call Uma shows me her photo album. One of the few people I have met being in possession of such an item, Uma stores this album in a safe place away from the reach of the other residents. Going through the pages with her I learnt about Uma's history and also learnt more about her relationship to the world of images. I filmed such conversations attempting to gather details of both the image and of her expressions (a difficult task indeed).

Finally let me add that I seldom allow myself to stay out of the images that I made. I have an avalanche of selfies and of portraits made of me together my interlocutors (Fig. 19).

And conventionally I also allowed myself to become the object of our filmed conversations (Fig. 20). Inverting the relationship between interviewer and interviewee I generally told my stories and my reflections on death, grief and love hence triggering off the reactions of my interlocutors. This led to the discovery of the kindness and compassion of the people I met and of their desire to offer me guidance in my life choices. Characterized by what I call 'ethics of inversion', these shared storytelling moments turned me (the observer) into part of what is to be observed. Such images, like all the images I made during fieldwork, were shared with my interlocutors. Considering them a common belonging I sent the images to them via WhatsApp or via other means. In the case of Mokshdhamas, I also made a promo for marketing the home.

Fig. 18. Portrait of Uma Aunty. *Source:* Photo by Paolo Silvio Harald
Favero.

Fig. 19. Selfie With Slimy Sid. *Source:* Photo by Paolo Silvio Harald
Favero.

Fig. 20.   Me With Slimy Sid. *Source:* Photo by Paolo Silvio Harald Favero.

7. CONCLUSIONS

My explorations of death in Delhi developed (and still develops) along a continuum of mediations. From the body to the camera, the sound recorder, the
smartphone and the computer screen. Each of these technologies of mediation
has given me access to a different layer of understanding, of comprehension.
Analysing online spaces, I did gather a precious view from above (a macro view)
of the key dimensions and concerns that surround the question of death in Delhi.
I identified key waves of concern for it amidst a city that peacefully co-exists with
death. The smartphone functioned as the link between the online and the offline.
Its apps, camera and note-taking affordances brought the digital straight down
into the terrane, material contact with everyday life, supporting and guiding me
in my daily actions. The smartphone expanded my own body–mind complex, and
its capacity for perception, interception/introspection and proprioception. The
camera, a key actor, became part of this choreography partly as a detached eye
partly also as a tool (inspired by my own 'ethics of exposure') igniting people's
desire to chat. And the smartphone, again, brought these stories back to the
people I was doing my research with.

All together these different mediations, and the use of an 'expanded' ethnographic approach, have given me access to different layers of connection to the
topic of death in Delhi and also to my ageing guides/interlocutors. Some of the
experiences that I collected are not a matter of interpretive knowledge per se.
They have more to do with the sphere of empathy, of (co-)presencing and
compassion. In addressing compassion here, however, I do not intend to speak of
it as a moral category, as an attainable gesture, a virtuous trait of the human
character. Etymologically coming from the Latin term *compassio* ('suffering
with') which in turn is a loan translation from Greek *sympatheia* (sympathy),
compassion is an experiential category that is the object of much research today

in the neurosciences. It is part of the embedded traits of our consciousness as human beings. Compassion is today more and more identified by the neurosciences as a key emotion guiding the understanding of what Einstein labelled as the 'intuitive mind' or what we could call the non-verbal mind. Rather than addressing details and logic, this is the part of our awareness that is interested in grasping simultaneously the whole picture. It grants us access to the corporeal, affective experience of being alive, in all its varied shapes. The camera manages to express this form of understanding better than verbal explanations. It takes us straight into that terrain where the know-able and the be-able meet.

REFERENCES

Abu-Lughod, L. (1991). Writing against culture. In R. G. Fox (Ed.), *Recapturing anthropology: Working in the present*. Santa Fe: School of American Research Press.

Agar, M. H. (1996). *The professional stranger* (2nd ed.). New York, NY: Academic Press.

Albers, P., & James, W. (1988). Travel photography. A methodological approach. *Annals of Tourism Research*, *15*(1), 134–158. doi:10.1016/0160-7383(88)90076-X

Bhatia, G. (1994). *Punjabi Baroque and other memories of architecture*. New York, NY: Penguin.

Byung-Chul, H. (2022). Retrieved from https://artreview.com/byung-chul-han-i-practise-philosophy-asart/#:~:text=Byung%2DChul%20Han%20is%20a,found%20traction%20as%20well%20scpticism

Chaudhuri, U. (2016, April 17). The fifth wall: Climate change dramaturgy. Retrieved from https://howlround.com/fifth-wall

Favero, P. (2003). Phantasms in a "Starry" place: Space and identification in a central New Delhi market. *Cultural Anthropology*, *18*(4), 551–584.

Favero, P. (2005). *India dreams: Cultural identity among young middle class men in New Delhi*. Stockholm Studies in Social Anthropology. Stockholm University Press.

Favero, P. S. H. (2013). Picturing life-worlds in the city: Notes for a slow, aimless and playful visual ethnography. *Archivio Anthropologico del Mediterraneo*, *16*(2), 33–48. Annno XVII.

Favero, P. (2017). In defence of the "thin": Reflections on the intersections between interactive documentaries and ethnography. In E. Gómez Cruz, S. Sumartojo, & S. Pink (Eds.), *Refiguring techniques in digital visual research* (pp. 51–65). London: Palgrave.

Favero, P. S. H. (2018). *The present image: Visible stories in a digital habitat*. London: Palgrave Macmillan.

Favero, P. S. H. (2020). *Image-Making-India: Visual culture, digital technologies and the politics of everyday life in a changing country*. London: Routledge.

Geertz, C. (1973). Thick description: Toward an interpretive theory of culture. In *The interpretation of cultures: Selected essays* (pp. 3–30). New York, NY: Basic Books.

Gramsci, A. (1971). *Selections from the prison notebooks*. London: Lawrence and Wishart.

Hine, C. (2015). *Ethnography for the internet: Embedded, embodied and everyday*. London: Bloomsbury Academic.

Horst, H. A., & Miller, D. (2012). *Digital anthropology* (1st ed.). London: Routledge.

Ingold, T. (2004). Culture on the ground: The world perceived through the feet. *Journal of Material Culture*, *9*(3), 315–340.

Jain, A. K. (1990). *The making of a metropolis: Planning and growth of Delhi*. Delhi: National Book Organisation.

Kaviraj, S. (1997). Filth and the public sphere: Concepts and practices about space in Calcutta. *Public Culture*, *10*(1), 83–113.

Lehmuskallio, A. (2019). The look as a medium: A conceptual framework and an exercise for teaching visual studies. *Journal of Visual Literacy*, *38*(1–2), 8–21.

Levinas, E. (1987). *Time and the other* [Richard A. Cohen Trans.]. Pittsburgh: Duquesne University Press.

MacDougall, D. (1997). The visual in anthropology. In M. Banks & H. Morphy (Eds.), *Rethinking visual anthropology* (pp. 276–295). New Haven, CT: Yale University Press.

McLuhan, M. (1994). *Understanding media: The extensions of man.* Cambridge, MA: The MIT Press.

Narayan, K. (1993). How native is a "native" anthropologist? *American Anthropologist, 95*(3), 671–686. Retrieved from http://www.jstor.org/stable/679656

Niebauer, C. (2019). *No self no problem: How neuropsychology is catching up to Buddhism.* San Antonio, TX: Hierophant Publishing.

Pauwels, L. (2015). The mimetic mode: From exploratory to systematic visual data production. In *Reframing visual social science.* Cambridge: Cambridge University Press.

Singh, K. (1990). *Delhi: A novel.* New Delhi: Penguin.

Stoller, P. (1989). *The taste of ethnographic things: The senses in anthropology.* Philadelphia, PA: University of Pennsylvania Press.

Chapter 7

ISOLATED BUILDINGS AS INDICATORS OF SOCIAL CHANGE, A VISUAL ESSAY

David Schalliol

ABSTRACT

This chapter introduces "Isolated Building Studies," a photographic series that interrogates Chicago's landscape of racial and economic segregation. In order to facilitate comparison, the series features uniform compositions of buildings that do not have neighboring structures. Through the repetition of these buildings and their uncanny settings, viewers are pushed to investigate relationships between these scenes and the social, political, and economic forces that created them.

Keywords: Cities; built environment; deindustrialization; gentrification; social stratification; segregation

Since 2006, I have been working on "Isolated Building Studies," a visual and public sociological project for which I photograph Chicago buildings using a uniform composition. Each of the more than 700 photographs in the series features a single building centered in the frame, flanked by parcels without structures (For example, see Fig. 1).

I started the project as a new way to conceptualize the physical effects of investment and divestment in the starkly racially and economically segregated city of Chicago. Of course, there has been serious attention directed to the city and its inequities, from early work of scholars like W. I. Thomas, Ernest Burgess, Jane Addams, and others affiliated with the first Chicago School;

Visual and Multimodal Urban Sociology, Part B
Research in Urban Sociology, Volume 18B, 171–184
Copyright © 2023 by Emerald Publishing Limited
All rights of reproduction in any form reserved
ISSN: 1047-0042/doi:10.1108/S1047-00422023000018B007

Fig. 1.   Isolated Building Study 288 (2008).

scholars of the second Chicago School, like Gerald Suttles, Arnold Hirsch, and Richard Taub; and research launched by Williams Julius Wilson, Robert Sampson, and their students, including Mary Pattillo, Sudhir Venkatesh, and Loïc Wacquant.

In addition to this sociological research is more public-facing work, including a group of powerful projects about public housing in 1990s Chicago, especially the books *There are No Children Here* (Kotlowitz, 1992) and *Our America* (Jones et al., 1998) and the films *Hoop Dreams* (James, 1994) and *Public Housing* (Wiseman, 1997). Perhaps the most important sustained visual project started in the late twentieth century is Camilo Vergara's oeuvre, which foregrounds repeated photographs of locations over decades to conceptualize the physical changes underway in the city's most structurally disadvantaged communities (see: Vergara, 1995, 2005; Vergara & Samuelson, 2001). Into the twenty-first century, artists including filmmaker Ronit Bezalel (see: Bezalel, 2015), photographer and community activist Tonika Lewis Johnson (see: Johnson, 2018), filmmaker and photographer Carlos Javier Ortiz (see: Ortiz, 2014), and visual artist Amanda Williams (see: Williams, various dates) have continued this public conversation about how to understand and address Chicago's fragmented inequality.

There is much to discuss.

Today, city residents often simplify Chicago into the North, South, and West Sides, with Lake Michigan taking the place of a proper East Side. The North Side

Table 1. Characteristics of Three Chicago Neighborhoods, Compared to City Averages 2015–2019.

	Median Household Income	% Black	% White	% Hispanic	% Asian	% Other	% Vacant Housing Units	% Vacant Land Use in 2015[a]
Chicago[b]	$58,247	29.2%	33%	28.8%	6.5%	2.2%	12.2%	5%
Austin[c]	$33,515	77.8%	5.6%	15.1%	0.5%	1.1%	14.3%	4.7%
Englewood[d]	$22,127	94.6%	0.6%	3.7%	0.3%	0.8%	34.9%	22.5%
Lincoln Park[e]	$115,389	4.9%	78.7%	6.2%	7.2%	2.2%	8.5%	1.5%

[a]Chicago Metropolitan Agency for Planning (2020).
[b]Chicago Metropolitan Agency for Planning (2021d).
[c]Chicago Metropolitan Agency for Planning (2021a).
[d]Chicago Metropolitan Agency for Planning (2021b).
[e]Chicago Metropolitan Agency for Planning (2021c).

is understood to be the wealthier, whiter, and denser part of the city to the poorer, predominately Latinx and Black South and West Sides. Using the most recent data from the United States Census Bureau's American Community Survey and analysis by the Chicago Metropolitan Agency for Planning, three well-known Chicago neighborhoods are instructive examples. As seen in the table below, the West Side Austin neighborhood is 77.8% Black, with a median household income of $33,515. 14.3% of the neighborhood's dwellings are vacant, while 4.7% of the parcels are vacant. On the South Side, Englewood is nearly 95% Black, with a median household income of $22,127. 34.9% of its dwellings are vacant, while 22.5% of its parcels are vacant. The North Side Lincoln Park community area is approximately 79% white, with a median household income of $115,389. Only 8.5% of its housing units are vacant, while 1.5% of the parcels are vacant (Table 1).

The economic and racial segregation that divides the city is unquestionably connected to the physical environment, an association that was exacerbated during the 2007–2009 financial crisis. During the Great Recession, neighborhoods on the South and West Sides of the city endured the highest foreclosure rates in the city. For example, in 2007, Englewood experienced nearly 90 foreclosure starts per square mile, second only to its neighbor West Englewood. In comparison, Lincoln Park had approximately one-eighth the number, with 11 starts per square mile (Young, 2008). Among other consequences, these foreclosures ultimately resulted in hundreds of additional demolitions in the city's South and West Sides than on its North Side.[1]

---

[1]Author's analysis of demolition permits from City of Chicago (2021).

As a sociologist who works in photography and film, I wanted to more clearly unite these sociological and public approaches to understanding the magnitude of Chicago's inequities. While I was already contributing to that established body of work about public housing, I wanted to bolster the scant attention directed toward understanding how segregation was affecting residential neighborhoods and commercial corridors throughout the South and West Sides.[2]

The physical isolation of small residential and commercial buildings is a potent vehicle to explore inequality and neighborhood change because the structures are at odds with their immediate surroundings. Their form illustrates their architects' constrained and intended relationships with adjacent structures. Typically, the buildings are boxy, multistory structures that are taller than they are wide. They maximize their interior floorspace by nearly filling the width of their narrow parcels. They are urban buildings. But when their neighbors are missing, a tension emerges: the urban form clashes with the seemingly suburban, even rural, setting. By horizontally photographing the principal elevations of these vertical buildings, I emphasize their relationship with the surrounding streetscape, particularly the "vacant" adjacent parcels. My intention is to foreground this tension within each photograph and prompt an initial question: "Why is this building isolated?"

The photographed details may help viewers answer this question. In the case of older structures – which may be discernible by their brickwork, ornamentation, and (often) the patina of neglect – remnants of previous neighbors may be visible: an uneven side wall, an arch that terminates before it reaches its terminus, or a fence dividing claimed and seemingly unclaimed territory (For example, see Fig. 2). These physical details illustrate a history of construction and, then, near destruction. In the case of newer structures – which are typically identified by pristine but unadorned façades, window-heavy designs, and new construction materials – the gradual accumulation of historical action is ruptured, suggesting wholesale change (For example, see Fig. 3).

Each of these buildings tells us about the history and present of the community and may also help us infer the future. The tension is not only situated in the reading of landscape elements as old and new, in place and out of place. The underlying tension is that isolated buildings occupy a certain duality of transformation: with the dissolution of one community comes the creation of another. Whether a building is a pioneer or a survivor, built by gentrification or decayed by divestment, these buildings and their environs demonstrate how inequitably structured investment cycles affect our built environment, urban neighborhoods, and community relationships.

I desired to express the enormity and importance of these changes through the scale of the typological project. Rather than simply share a few

Fig. 2. Isolated Building Study 205 (2007).

Fig. 3. Isolated Building Study 400 (2009).

photographs of isolated buildings, my installations of the series typically include dozens of images. One consequence of this decision is that the above patterns can be clarified by recontextualizing them from their given environments into an abstracted neighborhood of isolated buildings in a gallery (see: Chicago Architecture Biennial, 2015; DePaul Art Museum, 2013; Museum of Contemporary Photography, 2019; Pinkcomma Gallery, 2015) or publication (see: Mahall & Serbest, 2009; Schalliol, 2014). In so doing, new construction and old, homes and businesses, rich neighborhoods and poor neighborhoods are placed side by side. Judging by the conversations made while observing these installations, viewers are thus pushed to investigate relationships, to delve into common histories and reveal the political and economic forces leading to isolation. This new method of seeing alters not only how we interpret what we perceive but also which questions are raised. Instead of seeing one peculiar building, we see the legacy and immediacy of urban transformation. Instead of asking "What happened to *this* house?" we ask "What is causing this phenomenon?" (For example, see Figs. 4–16).

Fig. 4.   Isolated Building Study 230 (2007).

Fig. 5. Isolated Building Study 139 (2007).

Fig. 6. Isolated Building Study 412 (2007).

Fig. 7.   Isolated Building Study 640 (2014).

Fig. 8.   Isolated Building Study 593 (2012).

Fig. 9. Isolated Building Study 570 (2012).

Fig. 10. Isolated Building Study 590 (2012).

Fig. 11.   Isolated Building Study 519 (2007).

Fig. 12.   Isolated Building Study 657 (2016).

Fig. 13. Isolated Building Study 127 (2007).

Fig. 14. Isolated Building Study 701 (2019).

Fig. 15.   Isolated Building Studies, Various Dates (2006–2023).

Fig. 16.   Isolated Building Studies, Various Dates (2006–2023).

REFERENCES

Bezalel, R. (Director). (2015). *70 Acres in Chicago: Cabrini Green*. Ronit Films.
Bloom, N. D., Lasner, M. G., & Schalliol, D. (2016). *Affordable housing in New York City*. Princeton, NJ: Princeton University Press.
Chicago Architecture Biennial. (2015). BOLD Group Exhibition. Chicago, IL.

Chicago Metropolitan Agency for Planning. (2020). 2015 land use inventory. Retrieved from https:// datahub.cmap.illinois.gov/dataset/land-use-inventory-for-northeastillinois-2015. Accessed on September 30, 2021.

Chicago Metropolitan Agency for Planning. (2021a). Chicago community area series: Austin community data snapshot. Retrieved from https://www.cmap.illinois.gov/documents/10180/126764/ Austin.pdf. Accessed on September 30, 2021.

Chicago Metropolitan Agency for Planning. (2021b). Chicago community area series: Englewood community data snapshot. Retrieved from https://www.cmap.illinois.gov/documents/10180/ 126764/Englewood.pdf. Accessed on September 30, 2021.

Chicago Metropolitan Agency for Planning. (2021c). Chicago community area series: Lincoln Park community data snapshot. Retrieved from https://www.cmap.illinois.gov/documents/10180/ 126764/Lincoln+Park.pdf. Accessed on September 30, 2021.

Chicago Metropolitan Agency for Planning. (2021d). Municipality series: Chicago community data snapshot. Retrieved from https://www.cmap.illinois.gov/documents/10180/102881/Chicago.pdf. Accessed on September 30, 2021.

City of Chicago. (2021). Chicago data portal: Building permits table. Retrieved from https://data. cityofchicago.org/Buildings/Building-Permits/ydr8-5enu. Accessed on September 30, 2021.

DePaul Art Museum. (2013). Histories/photographies group exhibition. Chicago, IL.

James, S. (Director). (1994). *Hoop Dreams* [Film]. Kartemquin Films.

Johnson, T. L. (2018). *Folded map project*. Retrieved from http://www.foldedmapproject.com. Accessed on September 30, 2021.

Jones, L., Newman, L., & Isay, D. (1998). *Our America: Life and death on the South Side of Chicago* (Reprint ed.). Scribner.

Kotlowitz, A. (1992). *There are no children here: The story of two boys growing up in the other America* (1st ed.). Doubleday.

Mahall, M., & Serbest, A. (2009). *How architecture learned to speculate*. Gerd de Bruyn for Institut Grundlagen moderner Architektur und Entwerfen, Universität Stuttgart.

Museum of Contemporary Photography. (2019). Chicago stories: Carlos Javier Ortiz and David Schalliol. Dual Exhibition. Chicago, IL.

Ortiz, C. J. (2014). *We all we got*. Red Hook Editions.

Pinkcomma Gallery. (2015). Typology and change. Solo Exhibition. Boston, MA.

Schalliol, D. (2012). A method of living. *Places Journal*. Retrieved from https://placesjournal.org/ article/a-method-of-living/. Accessed on March 16, 2022.

Schalliol, D. (2014). Isolated building studies. UTAKATADO.

Schalliol, D. (2017). The Plan for Transformation has transformed Chicago's built environment. *Chicago Reader*. Retrieved from https://chicagoreader.com/newspolitics/the-plan-for-transformation-has-transformed-chicagos-built-environment/. Accessed on March 16, 2022.

Vergara, C. J. (1995). *The new American Ghetto*. New Brunswick, NJ: Rutgers University Press.

Vergara, C. J. (2005). *How the other half worships*. New Brunswick, NJ: Rutgers University Press.

Vergara, C. J., & Samuelson, T. (2001). *Unexpected Chicagoland* (First Printing ed.). New York, NY: The New Press.

Williams, A. (Various dates). Color(ed) theory. Retrieved from https://awstudioart.com/section/ 373029-Color-ed-Theory-Series.html. Accessed on September 30, 2021.

Wiseman, F. (Director). (1997). *Public Housing*. Zipporah Films.

Young, S. (2008). *The foreclosure crisis in the Chicago area: Facts, trends and responses*. DePaul University Real Estate Center.

INDEX